Schriften zur
Europäischen Integration und
Internationalen Wirtschaftsordnung

Veröffentlichungen des
Wilhelm Merton-Zentrums für Europäische Integration und
Internationale Wirtschaftsordnung

edited by

Professor Dr. Dr. Rainer Hofmann, Universität Frankfurt a. M.
Professor Dr. Stefan Kadelbach, Universität Frankfurt a. M.
Professor Dr. Rainer Klump, Universität Frankfurt a. M.

Volume 74

Stefan Kadelbach | Rainer Hofmann [eds.]

European Democracy and Public Sphere

Nomos

Onlineversion
Inlibra

The Deutsche Nationalbibliothek lists this publication in the Deutsche Nationalbibliografie; detailed bibliographic data are available on the Internet at http://dnb.d-nb.de

ISBN 978-3-7560-3607-3 (Print)
978-3-7489-6762-0 (ePDF)

1st Edition 2026

Preface

Signs of a deterioration of democratic culture can currently be observed in various member states of the European Union. The 23rd Walter Hallstein-Symposium that took place on 21 and 22 March 2024 at Goethe University in Frankfurt was dedicated to European democracy and the public sphere in light of the 2024 elections to the European Parliament.

The topic is multi-layered and not limited to jurisprudence. The symposium therefore took a multifaceted approach with speakers from various member states and with different disciplinary perspectives. Thus, a historian of political ideas from both Britain and France (*Niall Bond*, Lyon), a Member of the European Parliament (*Sven Simon*, Strasbourg/Marburg), a constitutional comparatist of Hungarian origin working in Germany (*Kriszta Kovács*, Berlin), a jurist, former politician and ambassador for Poland to Austria (*Irena Lipowicz*, Warsaw), a constitutional lawyer from Italy (*Emilio Castorina*, Catania), and the president of the Supreme Administrative Court of Lithuania (*Skirgailė Žaltauskaitė-Žalimienė*, Vilnius) offered their insights into the interrelationship between political discourse, the functioning of democracy and its embeddedness in constitutional principles such as the rule of law and the protection of citizens' rights.

We should like to express our sincere gratitude, as always, to the Centre *Normative Orders* at Goethe University in Frankfurt as well as to the Chancellery of the State of Hesse and to the *Foundation for the Promotion of the International Relations* of Goethe University for their generous support to make the symposium possible. We also thank Raven Kirchner, Dr. Paul Lorenz, Malena Todt, Julian Knoch, Oskar Marx and Rebecca Strauch from the *Merton Centre for European Integration* at Goethe University for editing the manuscripts of the contributions to this volume.

The book mostly reflects the state of affairs as of August 2024, but was updated in some of its chapters.

Frankfurt am Main, summer 2025

Rainer Hofmann Stefan Kadelbach Rainer Klump

Table of Contents

Introduction: European Democracy and Public Sphere

Stefan Kadelbach and Rainer Hofmann

A. Threats to Democracy in Europe

Political discourse has changed in the past years. On the face of it, the development is due to the fact that populist forces are on the rise, but also that the new forms of communication by which political movements and parties compete for attention reward extremist positions, to the detriment of balanced approaches to problems to be solved. Oversimplified blueprints for solutions, false information, insults of the opponent, and manipulation have created a climate in which the formation of political will has become increasingly difficult. That those holding power too often do not adhere in the middle or long term to what they announced to do adds to a general and permanent state of uncertainty that has become a dominant sentiment in the public sphere.

The reasons are manifold. Factors that have contributed to the atmosphere are described for Poland by *Irena Lipowicz* in this volume in a way that can for the most part be projected to many societies in Europe.[1] Perhaps the most important reason is a general feeling of fear created by a political rhetoric of continuous disruption. Too many people see themselves on the dark side of globalisation. Technological change brought about by digitalisation result in overcharge on many counts. At the same time, public responsibility has been widely withdrawn, in pursuit of an ill-conceived economic governance of public services, and has often proven defunct, be it in health care, public transportation, social security, or education. Most of the European states are not able anymore to defend themselves sufficiently against threats to their internal or external security, be they of an economic, digital, military or hybrid nature.

One might think that joint efforts as they are possible in the framework of the European Union could at least help to address such shortcomings of the European state, not the least by providing funds as they were made

1 For Hungary see *Halmai*, The Hungarian Constitution in a European Perspective, in: Kadelbach (ed.), Verfassungskrisen in der Europäischen Union, 2018, p. 85.

available in response to the Covid pandemia and its aftermath. However, a contrary reaction has established political forces that make use of uncertainties by offering simple answers and by promising a way back to the so-called "good days". They appeal successfully to national pride of a retrospect type and blame all that is foreign for being responsible for crises and decay. Campaigns are directed against the weakest and against the state institutions that are designed to protect them. In states like Belgium, Finland, Hungary, Italy, The Netherlands, Sweden, and Slovakia, so-called populist, basically right-wing parties are governing, or participating in the government of, the country. This general climate has also played out in the last elections to the European Parliament.[2]

Once in power, as the cases of Hungary and Poland demonstrate, populist parties direct their activities against all institutions that could pose a counterweight against, or at least critically observe, their activities, such as an independent judiciary, free media, and institutions of higher education. In so doing, the claim to justification is democracy itself, since such forces tend to identify their will to hold and use power with the people's will.[3]

From a European perspective, the question is how the institutions of the European Union and European politics could cope with these challenges. In order to address this question, it does not seem superfluous to recall the Treaty framework and its limits for preserving the constitutional principles the developments just described threaten to erode. This is not simply an exercise to inquire into European powers to correct state politics to the better, but an effort to understand how well prepared the organisational structure is to safeguard its own values which, as Article 2 TEU runs, "*are common to the Member States in a society in which pluralism, non-discrimination, tolerance, justice, solidarity and equality between men and women prevail*", and on which its character as a "*community of law*"[4] based on these constitutional principles depends.

2 See European Parliament, 2024 European Election Results, https://results.elections.europa.eu/en/ (last access: 1 Aug 2025).

3 What today's common parlance would call populism complies with the definition of fascism by *Karl Loewenstein*, see *id.*, Legislative Control of Political Extremism in European Democracies, 38 Colum. L Rev. (1938) 591 (592 f. *et passim*).

4 *Hallstein*, Der unvollendete Bundesstaat, 1969, p. 33.

B. The Framework of the Treaties

The Founding Treaties contain several rules that deal with the interrelationship between the autonomy of state politics, the obligation of the member states to observe fundamental principles of the Union and democracy at the EU level. Taken together, they make limits visible that must not be overstepped if a state envisages to remain in the EU. In the case of conflict, the mechanism of Article 7 TEU and conciliatory procedures short of it can be put in place. Should a member find these limits too burdensome to observe, exit (Article 50 TEU) would be the only acceptable option.

To begin with, the Union is under an obligation to accept not only the equality of its member states, but also "*their national identities*" (Article 4 para. 2 TEU). That term can, by definition, not be subject to autonomous European interpretation. Thus, one might think that member states would be free to fill this concept, seemingly aiming at preserving a hard core of state sovereignty, by their own political will. However, as it is always the case with the *domaine reservé* of member states, those powers may not be exercised in a way as to violate European Union law. This means, on the one hand, that neither the European Court of Justice (ECJ) nor any other EU institution is in a position to define what the national identity of any member state might be. On the other hand, however, it is possible and legitimate for them to say which uses of state power do *not* count as a legitimate emanation of national identity. This constitutional minimum is what the so-called value clause of Article 2 TEU is meant to describe.

From this it follows that Article 2 TEU operates as a common minimum standard that informs the interpretation of the national identity clause of Article 4 para. 2 TEU. In that respect, the term "*European society*" used in Article 2 TEU might give rise to a misunderstanding, for it does not prescribe in a sociological sense a European "*leitkultur*" member states would have to accept. Rather, it sets out a core of normative elements that have to be present in a society and which must not be abandoned by any given government if it desires to stay in the Union. This understanding explains the reference to Article 2 in Article 7 TEU, which enshrines a procedure to be followed if a state breaks out of the common consensus, and in Article 49 TEU which incorporates Article 2 TEU as a requirement for accession.

Therefore, as *Kriszta Kovács* convincingly argues in her chapter in this book, the term "*national identity*" can only be a legal concept. As long as it is used by national courts and other institutions in a sense of "*consti-*

tutional identity", like the German Federal Constitutional Court or like the Lithuanian constitutional jurisprudence as described by *Skirgailė Žaltauskaitė-Žalimienė* in this book, it is in keeping with Article 4 para. 2 TEU, provided this constitutional identity does not contradict the common standard of Article 2 TEU.

Thus, it is, for instance, not justifiable under the national identity clause to revoke the independence of judges since it forms a core element of the rule of law and is a requirement of mutual trust in judicial cooperation between the member states, as the case-law on the so-called reform of the judiciary in Poland illustrates.[5]

This implies that such policies can likewise not be justified by the principle of democracy. Provided the national government and parliament have gained power in a way that satisfies fair democratic procedures, the rationale behind, however, is different. Even though the principle of checks and balances is not expressly mentioned in Article 2 TEU, it follows from the obligation to respect human rights that it encompasses the protection of the minority from the will of the majority. This obligation cannot be overruled by the principle of democracy.

A question that remains is whether the principle of democracy itself can be protected by the jurisprudence of the ECJ in the same way as the rule of law. So far, the Commission has not initiated infringement proceedings according to Article 258 TFEU because of a violation of the democracy principle as it did previously with respect to the rule of law, and the Court has not had the opportunity to rule on the matter. Recent case law indicates *obiter* that the ECJ might be inclined to do so.[6] However, it is difficult to tell what the bottom line for an acceptable democracy might be. Arguably, if large portions of a polity of, say, 10 per cent of the votes would be neglected in the composition of a national parliament or if the result of elections would prove false by international standards, this point could be reached.

For the time being, it appears worthwhile to reconsider – as it has continuously been done for decades – how far democracy in the European Union itself complies with such standards. Such self-reflection is not only mandatory for a system that adheres to constitutional standards, it is also necessary for being able to assess how far the system as it is can address the

5 Cf. *Wyrozumska*, Conflict between the Polish Constitutional Tribunal and the CJEU with regard to the reforms of the judiciary, 60 Archiv des Völkerrechts (2022) 379.

6 Cf. ECJ, *Commission v Malta* ("golden passports"), C-181/23, ECLI:EU:C:2025:283, paras. 89 and 94.

needs expressed by the outcome of European elections, be they comfortable or not. The task is not only to rethink the model of dual input legitimacy on which democracy in Europe rests, but also how to shape the election process of the Parliament and decision-making within its structure in order to bring outcomes in closer connection to the will of the electorate.

C. Approaches to the topic

The contributions in this book address the topic from different perspectives.

From a point of view of a historian of ideas, *Niall Bond* reflects on core concepts of European integration and the Treaties and what their theoretical origins are by starting from *Ferdinand Tönnies*' concepts of society and community. As is well known, the term "community" was used from the beginning to give the original organisations their names, such as the European Coal and Steel Community, the European Economic Community and the European Atomic Energy Community, whereas the term "society" appeared, as a core concept, only in the Lisbon Treaty (Article 2 TEU). There, "society" is described as an institution in which core values of the Union prevail.[7] Taken both notions together in terms of European law, it seems as if they have changed roles, compared to their meanings as they were used in *Tönnies'* sociology. The observation that the foundation of the Communities followed a Hobbesian idea to transfer powers in exchange for peace reinforces this view. Other terms taken up in *Bond*'s contribution are sovereignty, *leitkultur*, and solidarity, all of which are commonly associated with societies, or communities, for that matter, within a state. Whether they can be transferred one day to Europe as a whole depends on the willingness of state governments and polities to let this happen.

That strong political currents point into a different direction and how some forces in state politics use "Europe" as a profile of the enemy is demonstrated by the Polish example by *Irena Lipowicz*. She shows which historical contingencies have contributed in parts of the Polish society to a climate that is hostile to the political class, independent state institutions, and free media. As in some other member states, political action used

7 When it comes to representation, the Treaties speak of "*civil society*", see Article 11 para. 2 TEU ("*dialogue*" with EU institutions) and Article 302 para. 2 TFEU („*civil society*" which the Economic and Social Committee shall consult).

and reinforced this atmosphere and aimed at everything that is meant to restrict ensuing authoritarian tendencies which, in turn, touches fundamental principles that constitute preconditions for becoming and being a member state of the European Union. From a European perspective, there are four threads along which these developments can be addressed; they are laid out in the following chapters.

A first approach would start from a presumption in favour of the powers of member states which underlies European Union policies and law, most clearly visible in the principle of conferral (Article 5 TEU). All powers not attributed to the Union remain in the hands of the member states. The identity clause already cited (Article 4 para. 2 TEU) makes it clear that the constituting elements of the member states shall be respected and remain beyond the reach of the use of Union powers. However, as *Kriszta Kovács* demonstrates in her chapter, the identity reservation is subject to abuse in that political actors claim their own political objectives to form part of national identity. Accordingly, a "thin layer" of governing principles marks the outer frontiers of what is acceptable within the European Union. To identify these limits is the purpose of Article 2 TEU, irrespective of the question how to come to terms with the concept of "society" used therein.

The second approach to define limits to unconstitutional national conduct starts from a traditional concept of the rule of law. On the one hand, the rule of law as such is to be preserved as a necessary corollary to European integration; to that end, various procedures under the threshold of Article 7 TEU have been put in place, such as the rule of law procedure and the justice barometer.[8] On a case-to-case basis, it is up to the judiciaries of the member states, the European Union and the Council of Europe to safeguard the rights of those who are affected by acts that go beyond rule of law standards. *Skirgailė Žalimienė* offers insights both from an academic and from a practitioner's point of view in the interaction between national and European courts, taking her home state Lithuania as an example.

A third approach is to take a look at the modes of democratic decision-making and, as a consequence, of the ability of problem-solving within the European Union. Thus, *Sven Simon* elaborates on questions of legitimacy and procedure which form the framework of how the European political

8 Cf. *Commission*, Communication: Strengthening the rule of law within the Union – A blueprint for action, COM 2019 (343) final; *Id.*, Communication: EU justice scoreboard, COM 2020 (306) final; see contributions to a former Hallstein Colloquium in *Kadelbach* (fn. 1).

system can react on political demands. It proves that the prospects for change are just open to progress as the member states want them to be and that Parliamentary ambitions remain caught between institutional restraints and the contingencies of political constellations.

An entirely different approach would be, fourthly and finally, to conceive identity as a common European concern. Not only would this open a perspective to see conflicts between different political factions within a member state and those between state governments and the European level as conflicts *within* a (European) society, without placing anyone outside of it.[9] Likewise, at an individual level, a European Union that cares about the needs of its Union citizens (Article 9 TEU) would gain legitimacy from a field that is crucial to acceptance of public authority, namely social rights. *Emilio Castorina* reflects on bad and good examples of European solidarity and projects republican notions of obligation and virtue to the ongoing task to come to terms with environmental degradation and climate change.

9 Cf. from a *Hegelian* perspective *von Bogdandy*, Strukturwandel des öffentlichen Rechts – Entstehung und Demokratisierung der europäischen Gesellschaft, 2022, pp. 16 ff.

What may have been meant by a European Community, and what are the consequences for a European normative political order?

Niall Bond

A. Introduction

I should like to thank the organisers of this meeting, Professor *Stefan Kadelbach* for the farsightedness and energy in bringing us all together, *Raven Kirchner*, who as the Goethe-University's law department's man in Lyon is the mediating proof of the usefulness of European programmes such as our university partnership *Minerve-Programme* with its potential for contributing to community, and *Patricia Psaila* for her generosity, efficiency and patience in making our arrival so smooth.

It is an honour to discuss meanings of the signifier "community" at a conference on *European Democracy and the Public Sphere* focussed on Europe engaging scholars from across the continent. *Walter Hallstein's* own "*Die europäische Gemeinschaft*"[1] places the notion of the community square in the centre of the discussion of a polity, but an understanding of the importance of grasping what was meant by *Gemeinschaft* seems to have been a foremost concern for the diplomat *Carl Friedrich Ophüls* (1895-1970)[2], whose role in the transition from an occupied status to that of a sovereign state with its historically problematic signifier *Volk* may have influenced his understanding both of community and democracy. Community is, in my view, a place in which a free but regulated public sphere allows for the democratic formation of common wills through respect, transparency, and allophilia, the embracing of outgroups and a readiness to make sacrifice for those who are different. The importance of outgroups, which are better protected in security communities, was incidentally stressed by the

1 *Hallstein*, Die Europäische Gemeinschaft, 1973. See also *Hallstein*, Zu den Grundlagen und Verfassungsprinzipien der Europäischen Gemeinschaft, in: Hallstein/Schlochauer (eds.), Zur Integration Europas – Festschrift für Carl Friedrich Ophüls, 1965, p. 1.

2 *Ophüls*, Zwischen Völkerrecht und staatlichem Recht. Grundfragen des europäischen Rechts, 4 Juristen-Jahrbuch 1963/64, 137.

political scientist *Karl Deutsch*[3] and distinguishes diametrically opposed conceptions of community.

Returning to the Forschungszentrum *Normative Orders* is serendipitous: many years ago, I met *Rainer Forst* here, and the expression "normative orders" inspired a piece I published on the notion of the community after a conference organised by the University of Buenos Aires and the Sorbonne.[4] Here, I shall defend the proposition that European integration has been built on at times contradictory, at times complementary normative orders of community and society that have served as inspiration for the title of a conference I am organising in Lyon in 2025 which I hope some of you shall attend. I have given it the title, *Les impensés de l'intégration européenne entre une communauté citoyenne et une société marchande* (*The imponderables of European integration between a community of citizens and market society*). As the Polish European MP *Bronislaw Gerenek* noted in his contribution to the anthology *What holds Europe together*[5], "*The debate on 'union'* must now be accompanied by a debate on '*community*.'" Here, I shall argue that in their pursuit of an at the time utopian dream the predominantly French and German founders of European integration who attempted to create a community rather than merely a society in Europe through what *Robert Schuman* described as a solidarity of facts, drew from a canon of political, economic and social thought that through intertwined intricacy leads us through preeminent and in certain respects unspeakable political movements back to philosophers whose legacy can be unravelled to consider the opportunities and risks of the project of European integration. I shall be speaking above all as an historian of political and social ideas.

B. The meaning of the European Community

In his history of the origins of European integration published in 2012 by the political scientist *Antonin Cohen* entitled *De Vichy à la Commu-*

3 *Deutsch*, Political Community at the International Level. Problems of Definition and Measurement, 1954.

4 *Bond*, Comunidad y normatividad en las ciencias sociales y humanas, Diferencia(s): revista de teoría social contemporánea, vol. 1, no. 14 (2022), 11

5 *Geremek*, Thinking about Europe as a Community, in: Michalski (ed.), What holds Europe together?, 2006, p. 5.

nauté européenne[6], essential parts of which were summed up in his contribution, "*When the Dream (Almost) Came True: European Community from Ideology to Institutions*" to a book I have edited for *Brill* on *The Concept of Community from a Global Perspective*[7], he has shown us how the project of a supranational authority presiding over a market economy (with subsisting elements of cartels) remote from parliamentary control drew from personalist and communitarian third way ideology that rejected both capitalism and socialism, presenting the founding acts of European construction not so much as an origin but as a conclusion. The origins of the collocation the Third Way, which was neither the invention of Mr. *Blair* nor Monsieur *Macron*, and which their spin doctors are hardly likely to emphasize, are to be found according to *Cohen's* genealogy of discourses of European integration in the European movement of fascism with its rejection of the divisiveness of the timocratic rule of parliament and the market. We are reminded that alongside the *Begriffsgeschichte* of community or *Gemeinschaft*, we could pursue an equally unsettling conceptual history of democracy in a territory which includes the vestiges of by the standards of Copenhagen anything but democratic culture of the German Democratic Republic. Looking further back to the time of *Walter Hallstein's* first appointment as a lecturer of law here in Frankfurt, we can find a yet more incongruous understanding of *Volksherrschaft*.

Cohen's groundbreaking work breaks with the historical tradition of presenting European integration in France as the sole brainchild of the resistance movement, instead highlighting the ideological legacy of Vichy, which itself drew from a work by the founder of sociology in Germany, *Ferdinand Tönnies*, entitled *Gemeinschaft und Gesellschaft*. For *Tönnies'* conceptual, on occasions Manichean opposition exercised a charismatic sway outside incipient sociology notwithstanding *Tönnies'* fervid opposition to fascism and national socialism, and to his rejection of the "*sich klugdünkende Nützanwendungen*"[8] ("*would-be clever applications*" – transl. by the author) of his concepts (particularly community or more notably folk community, *Volksgemeinschaft*), and his courageous rejection of the personality of *Adolf Hitler*. *Tönnies'* very public opposition to *Hitler* meant

6 *Cohen*, De Vichy à la Communauté européenne, 2012.

7 *Cohen*, When the Dream (Almost) Came True: European Community from Ideology to Institutions, in: Bond (ed.), The Concept of Community from a Global Perspective, 2024, p. 125.

8 *Tönnies*, Gemeinschaft und Gesellschaft, 1880-1935, vol. 2, in: Clausen/Haselbach (eds.), Ferdinand Tönnies Gesamtausgabe, 2019, p. 29 and p. 116.

that at the end of his life following the seizure of power by the Nazis, he was ejected from the civil service and lost his pension, leading him to a situation of marginalisation reminiscent of that he had suffered in his early career, when he was discriminated against in his academic career due to his defence of left-wing causes, notably that of organised labour. His pleas that during the First World War, he had defended national preference – for he had been a propagandist for the Second Reich – fell on the deaf ears of the Nazi bureaucrats, as his reputation for sympathies for social democracy, Enlightenment and certain shared assumptions of liberalism was indelible.

As a Europeanist I am specialized less in the political sociology of European institutions – which I came to know most when I attended meetings as an interpreter at the European Central Bank here in Frankfurt, which inspired me to set up a *Jean Monnet* action plan drawing from that experience – than in the history of the denotative and just as importantly connotative implications of concepts – those of politics, economics, sociology, and law in Europe. My conviction of the importance of understanding their historical developments was influenced by *Reinhard Koselleck*, influenced by the legal thinker *Carl Schmitt*, whose National Socialist career and own opportunistic definition of democracy have obscured his contribution to making clear the murkiness of concepts. As *Nietzsche* wrote, "*Definierbar ist nur das, was keine Geschichte hat*"[9] ("*only what has no history can be defined*" – transl. by the author).

Legal thinkers from whom *Tönnies* drew illuminate through their juxtaposition the opposition between community and society: the dogmatically utilitarian *Rudolf von Jhering*, whose "*Der Zweck im Recht*" of 1877[10], translated and published in English as "*Law as a Means to an End*"[11] in 1913, was a source of inspiration for *Tönnies*' understanding of *Gesellschaft* or Society, and supposed that the sole pursuit of self-interest was a preferable foundation for a functioning society than devotion to the others. Of an opposite mindset was *Otto von Gierke*, whose "*Rechtsgeschichte der deutschen Genossenschaft*"[12] of 1868, of which parts were translated and published in English in 1990 as "*Community in historical perspective*"[13], fed into *Tönnies*' concept of *Gemeinschaft* or community. For *Jhering* a society based upon

9 *Nietzsche*, Zur Genealogie der Moral, 1887, p. 71.
10 *Jhering*, Der Zweck im Recht, 1877.
11 *Jhering*, Law as a Means to an End, 1913.
12 *Gierke*, Rechtsgeschichte der deutschen Genossenschaft, 1868.
13 *Gierke*, Community in historical perspective, 1990.

spontaneous mutual generosity was a nightmare, and the marketplace with its individualistic pecuniary standards of equity a dream. Prior to 1870, *Gierke*, on the other hand, dreamed of Germany as a community of equals cleansed of the absolutist legacy of the French occupier, a Germany that would be united in a spirit of mutual fellowship and spontaneous association, prefiguring at a national level what Europeans were later to envisage on a continental level, and showing if need be that there were German roots and aspirations to truly democratic culture, understood by *Tocqueville* not as an institutional machine, but as a state of society. Another source of inspiration from the Law for *Tönnies* was that of a British jurist and historian, *Henry James Summer Maine*, whose Whig reading of history in "*Ancient Law: Its Connection with the Early History of Society, and Its Relation to Modern Ideas*"[14] published in 1861, with its argument that mankind has moved from status to contract, foreshadowed *Tönnies*' own philosophy of history of humankind in a for *Tönnies* inexorable movement from *Gemeinschaft* to *Gesellschaft*, from instinct to interest, and from love to purposive rationality. Arranged marriages that evolve towards harmony based upon mutual understanding are rare evidence that a double movement, a development in opposed directions is possible. The last seventy years of European integration have shown a movement from hostility or struggle to mutual toleration and in some instances to amity, countervailing criticisms of modernity which view the trend of human development as moving from compassion to selfishness.

European integration owed much to *Hobbes*' insight that without a sovereign in a Commonwealth, endowed by a social compact to quell inevitable strife arising from the concupiscent and irrational passions of humans, life would be "*nasty, short and brutish*".[15] In the aftermath of the Second World War, the insight was that without the pooling of sovereignty under a High Authority, the incomparably more violent strife of modern European nation-states labouring under the shadows of nuclear destruction would be deadly for the planet and our species, of which individuals and groups employ their rationality to ensure their own longevity and prosperity. Thus, postwar politicians sought to abolish *Hobbes*' state of nature at a world level through regional cooperation by mobilising utilitarianism

---

14 *Maine*, Ancient Law: Its Connection with the Early History of Society, and Its Relation to Modern Ideas, 1861.

15 *Hobbes*, Leviathan or The Matter, Forme and Power of a Commonwealth Ecclesiasticall and Civil, 1651, p. 88.

or the belief that individuals base all their decisions on the imminent obtention of pleasure or avoidance of pain the British philosopher *Jeremy Bentham* saw as what had come to be modernity's ubiquitous belief system.[16]

However, democracy, ancient and modern, has depended upon a degree of fellowship – one translation of *Gierke's Genossenschaft* – which can be seen as a readiness to do for one's fellow sentient creature, past, present, or future, something that would not reap us at least the equivalent in return. This readiness distinguishes what *Tönnies* saw as *Gemeinschaft* or community. If we consider *Tönnies'* definition of *Gesellschaft* as a state of affairs in which people are only prepared to give something that does not cost them more than what they have given, as was famously Mrs. *Thatcher's* approach to integration, we immediately understand why a European Community has to be something more than bread alone or a *sozialer Rechtsstaat.*

As *Tönnies* used them, the terms "*society*" or "*community*" are "*axiological operators*" – however apparently neutral, these terms contain normative injunctions. It may seem odd to present *Tönnies'* key sociological concepts as value judgments. After all, *Tönnies* had fought alongside *Max Weber* in the German Sociological Association to assert the importance of value neutrality in the social sciences, and *Tönnies* described the concepts *Gemeinschaft* and *Gesellschaft* first as "*normal concepts*" (which he identified as ideal types, or empirical descriptors). Yet anyone familiar with *Tönnies'* intellectual universe comes to realize that *Tönnies* has a clear preference for *Gemeinschaft* or Community over *Gesellschaft* or Society, and he wrote to his wife that he loathed *Gesellschaft* and loved *Gemeinschaft.* Beyond this personal preference, I argue that following *Arthur Schopenhauer*, we can and should see the study of ethics as the empirical study of outlooks and behaviour. The norms of modern market society were stated by *Adam Smith* in the revolutionary year 1776:

> "*It is not from the benevolence of the butcher, the brewer, or the baker, that we expect our dinner, but from their regard to their own interest. We address ourselves, not to their humanity but to their self-love, and never talk to them of our own necessities but of their advantages.*"[17]

---

16 *Bentham*, An Introduction to the Principles of Morals and Legislation, 1789.

17 *Smith*, An Inquiry into the Nature and Causes of the Wealth of Nations, 1776, cited following Campbell/Skinner (eds.). The Glasgow Edition of the Works and Correspondence of Adam Smith, vol. II, 1976, p. 27.

In another revolutionary year 1789, the philosopher *Jeremy Bentham* had published *An Introduction to the Principles of Morals and Legislation*, which announces that "*Nature has placed mankind under the governance of two sovereign masters, pain and pleasure*", arguing that "*it is for them alone to point out what we ought to do, as well as to determine what we shall do. On the one hand the standard of right and wrong, on the other the chain of causes and effects, are fastened to their throne.*"[18] The "*principle of utility*" "*recognizes this subjection*" and aims to "*rear the fabric of felicity by the hands of reason and of law*"[19]. The utilitarian system, with its followers in law – I have already mentioned *Jhering* – and in the opposed camps of liberalism (such as *John Stuart Mill*) and socialism (e.g. *Robert Owens* and *Karl Marx*) described all law and the norms of reason derived from the individual pursuit of pleasure and avoidance of pain and the vision of all fellow creatures as serving or disserving these two ultimate motives, laying the foundations for the normative order of modern society. Various other philosophers such as *Adam Ferguson* explained how society became civil through the rise of rationalism.[20] The ultimate prescript remains to pursue your own interests, if needed at the expense of those of others, implying as *Smith* argued in a market that "*every man is a merchant*"[21] in the pursuit of advantages. A derivation from this constant pursuit of self-interest is social wealth and ultimately common good.

However, that normativity was countered by another, that of *Immanuel Kant* in the "*Groundwork for the Metaphysic of Morals*"[22] of 1785. Alongside the moral junction to act as if the maxim of your action were to become by your will a universal law of nature, *Kant* then goes on to the second formulation of the Categorical Imperative, "*Handle so, daß du die Menschheit sowohl in deiner Person als in der Person eines jeden anderen, jederzeit zugleich als Zweck, niemals bloß als Mittel brauchst*"[23] ("*So act that you use humanity, in your own person as well as in the person of any other, always at the same time as an end, never merely as a means.*")[24] These normative orders, if we read *Tönnies*, correspond to different spheres of the Law:

18 *Bentham* (fn. 16), p. i.
19 *Bentham* (fn. 16), p. i.
20 *Ferguson*, An Essay on the History of Civil Society, 1767.
21 *Smith* (fn. 17), p. 554.
22 *Kant*, Grundlegung zur Metaphysik der Sitten, 1785.
23 *Kant*, Grundlegung zur Metaphysik der Sitten, 1785, Bd. IV, p. 429.
24 Translation from *Gregor/Timmermann* (eds.), Immanuel Kant – Groundwork of the Metaphysics of Morals – A German-English Edition, 2012, p. 87.

Tönnies saw the explicitly societal law, that of *Gesellschaft*, in commercial law with its commutative ideal of justice and that of *Gemeinschaft*, communitarian law, in family law, with its distributive ideal of justice. Thus, family law lays down preferences when dealing with relationships of community that do not apply to just any member of society. And in keeping with this principle, preferences, often economic, are attributed to communities – to the community of the nation, or to Europe, as in the European context the expression "Community preference", which is rarely regarded as offensive by those who get jittery when hearing the expression "national preference."

Community involves humans, or even more generally sentient creatures, around whom we orient our actions not just to further our own interests, but for whom we are prepared to make sacrifices without calculation. It involves the inequalities that are both empirically given, in our hearts and in our minds, that are not, as *Carl Schmitt* suggested in *Die geistesgeschichtliche Grundlage des heutigen Parlamentarismus*[25], immutable, but which call for remedial action. While *Gesellschaft* reposes upon awareness, bonds of *Gemeinschaft* presuppose that leap of faith which will not have us calculate profits and losses every time a transaction transpires.

This is a starting point for the discussion of community, at the levels of world governance, our politically organised continent, our nation states, regional and local authorities, and relationships with people we see on a day-to-day basis. The very idea of community is seen as fundamental for a democratic polity, even such democracies without a *demos* as the European Union. *Carl Schmitt* opined that democracy, of which inequality and fiction were irreducible aspects, essentially needed to be founded upon homogeneity – which has been interpreted as that of metaphysical belief or religion, culture, or indeed race. This opinion continues to inspire populist leadership in Europe, but the reality of the ethnic mix reduces such phantasies to a chimera. However, *representations* of ethnic homogeneity as a necessary source of community may come back to haunt us a century after Europe's conflagration. Germany's basic law laid down a loose framework of metaphysical beliefs necessary for coexistence in a *freiheitlich-demokratische Grundordnung*, a basic order of liberal democracy. In the quest of commonalities, Europe has laid down its own minimum standards in the Copenhagen Criteria[26] to anticipate the vastly differing meanings associated with

25 *Schmitt*, Die geistesgeschichtliche Lage des heutigen Parlamentarismus, 1923.
26 European Council in Copenhagen, Conclusions of the Presidency, (21-22 June 1993, SN 180/1/93).

the signifier democracy between long-standing liberal democracies of at least half a century of procedures and traditions and those political cultures that emerged after the collapse of *Realsozialismus*. And the Syrian-German *Bassam Tibi's* definition of culture corresponds not to what traditionally has been regarded as *Gemeinschaft*, but as *Gesellschaft* (*Tönnies'* words, not his), when he defended a European *Leitkultur*: "*The values needed for a core culture are those of modernity: democracy, secularism, the Enlightenment, human rights and civil society.*"[27] In so doing, he addressed a meaning of integration that it is not so commonly linked to the European integration of markets, of nation states and of policy areas: he is implicitly evoking the gruelling integration of the initially outside, non-European world that made their entrance into Europe's cultures in the wake of colonialism, which has brought the European metropole both benefits and challenges. This is a reminder that a challenge for European democracy is the integration of outgroups and the dominated and a justice of reparation. However, it is my conviction that we must, in our understanding of cross-border, multi-level and geometrically variable governance go beyond those assumptions of *Tibi's Leitkultur* and find a greater readiness to mutual sacrifice, conditioned, of course, by respect.

In a debate on the pertinence of *Ferdinand Tönnies'* opposition of community and society in the construction of Europe at a workshop I organised on the idea of Europe in Lyon in 2019, polemics were sparked by *Antonin Cohen's* argument, since scrutinizing the 1940s is not as much a matter of course in France as it is in Germany, finding an affiliation of the ideal of European federalism in the murky camp of fascism is distasteful, and certain scholars still prefer to conceive of the Schuman declaration as a beginning and not the end of a historical development. (That *Tönnies* was a fervent opposition to National Socialism was not belaboured, inasmuch as his work may seem to have provided grist to the mill of blood and soil interpretations of community, and notably by figures such as the economist *François Perrault*, who during the early 1940s drew from *Tönnies* to flesh out an ideological groundwork for the Vichy regime.) It was argued that the significance of "*communauté*" in opposition to "*société*" merely reflected *Jean Monnet's* determination to surmount the difficulties of international governance by eliminating the incapacity for decision-making so typical of the "*Société des Nations*" – the League of Nations (called not *Gesellschaft der Nationen* but *Völkerbund* in German). This was achieved by institut-

27 *Tibi*, Europa ohne Identität? Die Krise der multikulturellen Gesellschaft, 1998, p. 154.

ing a Higher Authority to which national leaders would have, by treaties instituted in a more Hobbesian than Romantic tradition, to yield. At stake was eliminating national veto rights, which were of course reinstated with the Luxemburg compromise and subsequently superseded. This reading of Community follows from a realism based upon the Hobbesian Commonwealth applied to nation states and utilitarianism applied to *homo europaeus.* But this reading seems to me to be an inadequate basis for the specific solidarity that underlies our communities and our acceptance of preferential behaviour which is antithetical to the individualistic optimisation of our chances on a market.

C. Consequences for a European normative political order

From the foregoing, we may ask ourselves whether community is a really operative factor of European politics. In the language of German classical social theory, alongside struggle or *Kampf* and society or *Gesellschaft*, i.e. the peaceable coexistence of humans upon assumptions rendered explicit in the term *Leitkultur*, community or *Gemeinschaft* is factually existent in everyday life, although *Tönnies* saw it to be merely latent from the advent of modernity onward (*wie Dornröschen in der verzauberten Burg*, like Sleeping Beauty in the enchanted fortress). *Tönnies* thought that everywhere, society supplanted community.

And yet, I would argue that the enchanting readiness to give without having calculated the possibility of receiving the equivalent – with vociferous exceptions such as Mrs. *Thatcher*, who is but one example of a consistent ideological approach from across the English channel – has been a constant of European integration. While consciousness (*Bewusstheit*) or awareness is a category of *Gesellschaft* or society, there must be a general acceptance of the flow of blood from one organ to another which keeps the organism alive, or a readiness to accept transfers as a consequence of the benefit of living in prosperity, while maintaining the principle of fiduciary and fiscal responsibility. Acceptance of community means accepting the controlled cost of European governance and programmes. *Gemeinschaft* or Community has a price. I do not think that Brexit has disproved this metaphor of the organism, inasmuch as there are many thriving amputees.

I would take up *Tönnies'* conception of community to show how pertinent he is to our discussion by referring to the speech in which, on

20 January 2013, *David Cameron* both defended his vision of a Europe united as a *Gesellschaft* or market – my words not his – while offering a referendum which would become Britain's undoing in Europe, a speech that appears in hindsight to be a sort of pre-amputation narcosis.[28] I choose to focus on one passage in his speech, when he declares: "*The map of global influence is changing before our eyes. And these changes are already being felt by the entrepreneur in the Netherlands, the worker in Germany, the family in Britain.*"[29] One of the foibles of *Tönnies' Community and Society* was the attempt to scientifically legislate the values of love by dictating to the reader to which individuals any given human will necessarily and therefore should privilege loyalty and devotion, and which categories of human beings are relegated to second place. For Mr. *Cameron*, the loyalty of other Britons is the family, *Gemeinschaft* or community.

An evocation of the family or the community suggests that Britain as the family was the legitimate place of unquestioning sacrifice or community preference. The Dutchman is a shrewd entrepreneur or manager of capital. It may be coincidence that Mr. *Cameron* mobilizes the classical economist *David Ricardo's* categories alongside the Netherlands when alluding to capital and labour; *Ricardo's* father had just moved from the Netherlands when *David* was born, and *Ricardo* had shown the importance of the role of capitalists in oiling the machine that guarantees the prosperity of individuals pursuing their interests on the market or in *Gesellschaft*. Of course, being able to make use of the efforts of a capitalist or of a labourer does not entail affection. Undiluted liberalism imposes the injunction to put up with market participants only so long as they provide you with advantage, and then walk off to the next, better-placed market participant. The worker in Germany is a reliably hard worker, who puts *Mercedes* into Tory garages. If Mr. *Cameron* was a one-nation Tory, he was certainly not a one-supernation European. His defence of Europe was in fact a defence of national preference. Yet how many British children felt Poles they encountered and were so stigmatized by the Leave Campaign were actually a bit nicer than their own family? In contradistinction to *Tönnies*, I would argue that Community can in fact be authentic even if its origins

28 *David Cameron's* speech can be found here: https://www.youtube.com/watch?si=Eys5jDORMRJv7Voz&embeds_referring_euri=https%3A%2F%2Fbritishheritage.org%2F&source_ve_path=Mjg2NjMsMjg2NjQsMTY0NTA2&v=ovFSiwmQq7o&feature=youtu.be (last access: 23 Oct 2025).

29 *Ibid.*

are contrived. Opportunities can be created for reciprocal knowledge and the building of trust, through the creation of European communities in the 1950s without consulting the Europeans, and through the deliberate creation of a European public sphere. This is so much easier to envisage now with the advancement of the language transformation tools of artificial intelligence. I believe *Jürgen Habermas* may be useful in reflecting on a European public sphere.[30]

Look half a century further back to another moment in thinking of community loyalties during the forging of the Elysée Treaty in 1963. *Charles de Gaulle* had called for a friendship between France and Germany that would, in the formulation of community by *Tönnies*, been exclusive living together, to the detriment to the UK as a potential member of the European family. The Bundestag responded famously with an ambivalent *Ja* (Yes) involving a preamble declaring UK Community membership and alliance with the United States in NATO to be aims complementary to their friendship with France. This was a declaration of non-preference for France, perhaps out of fear of manipulation, out of fear that when signing up for a friendship or *Gemeinschaft*, Germany might in fact be being manoeuvred into a *Gesellschaft*. This mitigated trust for France and equal trust for English-speaking partners – trust, I have shown elsewhere, is fundamental for community – contributed to Britain's entry into a community a decade to a month later.

Reciprocal knowledge of culture is vital for community to prosper. By culture I assume we understand that language is a prerequisite for community, and this is a reason to be concerned about the cooling off of that supranational *Liebäugeln* (flirting) still referred in France to as the French-German *couple*, a relationship in which the partners are decreasingly ready to invest time and effort in developing mutual knowledge. We can see that communities as they really exist, let's call them *Realgemeinschaften* in analogy to *Realsozialismus*, can be forged in balances of power and triangulations, and be at times held together by perceived threats from without and within. The idea that communities can be forged departs from *Tönnies*' assumption that communities pre-exist society as natural, or even biological entities and necessarily evolve with the development of individualist rational self-interest into societies. But I agree with *Tönnies* that

30 Esp. *Habermas*, Strukturwandel der Öffentlichkeit, 1962; *Habermas*, Ein neuer Strukturwandel der Öffentlichkeit und deliberative Politik, 2022.

they require trust that can only be developed through time and reciprocal familiarity.

As a historian of ideas, I follow *Antonin Cohen* that the understanding *Pierre Uri* may have had of community may have been derived from *Tönnies* and transformed under *Uri's* plume. *Pierre Uri* was a Frenchman of Jewish extraction and when France adopted the *Loi anti-juive* against the backdrop of the national revolution and the evocation of the national community, *Uri* defended the possible appurtenance to a multiplicity of communities. Thorough theoretical groundwork for this view had been laid by a German of Jewish extraction, *Tönnies'* acquaintance *Georg Simmel* during the 1890s. Now our multiplicity of community appurtenances – of blood, temperament, predisposition, belief systems, languages and cultural practices – is as cryingly obvious to modern Europeans as was the overwhelming belief in the legitimacy of the individual pursuit of maximum happiness was declared by *Bentham* to be when he elaborated his system of utilitarianism. European Integration has been a shift from Hobbesian realism to cultural allophilia, or a positive attitude to outgroup members, through a solidarity of daily deeds based upon myriad encounters and getting to know one another, whence the importance of cultural promotion in integration. The shift in an understanding of community from the assertion of a general will by a monolithic homogenous culture to a differentiated concertation of voices finds linguistic expression in a terminological shift the subtlety of which can be most readily appreciated in German. In 1887, *Tönnies* defined *Gemeinschaft* or community as "*Einheit in der Mehrheit*"[31] ("*unity in plurality*"). The present motto of the European Union is "*In der Vielfalt geeint*"[32] ("*united in diversity*").

Unity in diversity is achieved through the investment of the time needed for deeper mutual knowledge and less the peaceable settlement of differences in democracy as a theatre of conflict over the distribution of symbolic and material goods than their deliberate embracing in a spirit of recognition (*Anerkennung*), an idea fostered by *Axel Honneth* here in Frankfurt.[33] This unity in diversity is for me the salient distinction between a community of citizens as evoked by defenders of the French republican tradition

31 *Tönnies*, Gemeinschaft und Gesellschaft, 1887, S. 3.

32 https://european-union.europa.eu/principles-countries-history/symbols/eu-motto_de (last access: 23 Oct 2025).

33 *Honneth*, Kampf um Anerkennung, 1992.

such as *Dominique Schnapper*[34] and on the one hand a crushing and arbitrary imposition of the cultural standards of the dominant on an entire continent, or on the other a mere market society of juxtaposed individuals in the pursuit of their own immediate or postponed pleasure. This deeper mutual knowledge necessarily involves understanding diverse meanings associated with highly polysemous signifiers bandied about as unconsciously as democracy with their heavy normative implications. Again, we should heed *Nietzsche's* reminder that only those things that have no history can be defined. A word like democracy, just as a word like community, is by these standards irreducible to a terse definition, but presents a complexity of elements nourished by multiple strains of history which need to be critically explored and critically embraced because usage presents a grain of truth that has held sway over the living with their hearts and minds for a while during which it founded community – until such time as the consciousness and critical acumen of *Gesellschaft*, society tells us that it is time to move on. Community reposes upon intimate mutual understanding. This unity in diversity is what European governance must aim to achieve for the sake of the longevity of a democracy without a *demos.*

D. Democracy without a demos

What can popular sovereignty mean in the absence of a demos? If democracy reposes upon a fictitious identity between rulers linked to the political Copenhagen criteria – human rights, institutional stability, democracy and the rule of law and minority protection – *Monnet's* specific understanding of sovereignty as something which is more effective when it encompasses more than the people may give us a clue, borne out in the evolution within the treaties from rule by sovereign peoples to rule by sovereign citizens. To grasp popular sovereignty in the context of European integration, I suggest we draw from former President of the European Central Bank *Mario Draghi's* interpretation of *Jean Monnet's* idea behind the pooling of sovereignty: the intergovernmental concertation of policies in the presence of a mediating high authority meant not less but more sovereignty for participating nation-states.

34 *Schnapper*, La communauté des citoyens. Sur l'idée moderne de nation, 1994.

At the EU's coordination committee at the UN in Geneva I attended, the British voice was valued beyond the simple weight of the nation at those meetings inter alia due to the expertise of deft diplomats, and Britain's withdrawal from the EU has meant not so much the recovery of as the shattering loss of sovereignty. As *Draghi* pointed out when he was awarded the Gold Medal of the Fondation Jean Monnet in 2017, *Monnet's* focus was on effectiveness: "*Monnet's fundamental objective was to put governments back into a position to discharge their remit – meaning their capacity to ensure security, guarantee freedom, and create the conditions for the prosperity of their people.*"[35]

Supranational entities, nation-states, regions, *départements* or counties, and local authorities, but even individuals may be of a divided mind. De facto sovereignty means the ability to surmount this division of minds and opinion in order to act effectively. This sovereignty involves elements of *Hobbes'* Commonwealth, as well as understandings of both society and community.

The gradual transformation of our conception of popular sovereignty has evolved from the aim of the Treaty of Maastricht[36] to create an 'ever-closer union among the peoples of Europe', to omitting the notion of peoples in treatment of the European Parliament in the Treaty of Lisbon of 2007[37], in which pursuant to Article 14(2) of the Treaty on European Union (TEU), Parliament is now "*composed of representatives of the Union's citizens*", as opposed to representatives of 'the peoples of the States'. Pure national sovereignty diehards of motley political allegiances may have problems with this disappearance of a plurality of peoples and of a European people and their displacement by a diversity of citizens, however this is a realistic corollary of the plurality of appurtenances that characterizes multicultural European societies and underpins the mobility that makes mutual understanding – the basis for community – more probable.

The nurturing of a transnational civil society fully visible within the public sphere is vital for the fostering of a Europe-wide culture of the Union's citizens who gather together in transnational communities upon the basis of shared understandings and allophilia. Having crossed the border from France this morning, I feel some concern. It is true that government

35 *Draghi* is quoted here: https://www.ecb.europa.eu/press/key/date/2017/html/ecb.sp170504.en.html (last access: 23 Oct 2025).

36 Treaty on European Union [TEU – Maastricht Treaty], O.J. C 191/1.

37 Treaty of Lisbon – Amending the Treaty on European Union and the Treaty Establishing The European Community, O.J. C 306/1.

efforts at fostering mutual understanding between the couple that since 1951 has been at the heart of European integration – France and Germany – have been enormous. Such efforts have afforded me acquaintance with the organisers of this *Walter-Hallstein-Conference.* But mutual efforts at mutual understanding between France and Germany, notably among its youngest constituents, are waning. Whether *Monnet* actually said that were he to start again, he would have started with culture, mutual knowledge of culture and the culturally sacred enhances that sense of community that is vital for democracy throughout Europe.

Developments in Poland and their Consequences for the European Union

Irena Lipowicz

A. Introduction

Developments in Poland have aroused general interest in Europe in recent years. Conclusions were drawn – on the basis of the radical political turnaround after 2015 – that Poland, like Hungary, was setting a certain inevitable trend for the triumph of populism in Europe. This conviction was reinforced after the 2019 verdict was reached by the coalition of the *Law and Justice party* and the *Solidarity Poland SP party* in a second, victorious parliamentary term and the formation of a government. This meant a total of 8 years of rule by groupings actively contesting the foundations of the organization and functioning of the rule of law. This impact included institutional changes affecting all types of state bodies and functional changes interfering strongly with their mode of operation.[1] Let us try to outline their basic elements and reflect on the rationale for the unexpected political change of 2023 and their legal aspects.

B. New types of discontent

According to the Batory Foundation's research on populism in Central and Eastern Europe, the triumph of populism was a response – particularly in our region – to new types of discontent: including ontological, political and cultural discontent; it was linked to a distrust of the state – traditionally strong in Poland for historical reasons after long years of Partition and communist state oppression, and an acceptance of the promise of radical political change and described by those in power as "good change".[2]

1 *Barcz*, Niepraworządność w Polsce w świetle standardów unijnych. Wybór studiów i artykułów naukowych 2016-2023, 2024, p. 175 ff.

2 *Sadecka*, Zapotrzebowanie na populizm w ujęciu kulturowym. Niezadowolenie post transformacyjne i neo tradycjonalizm, in: Kubik (ed.), Populizm i demokracja – ro-

The elements present in Poland fulfilled all the basic conditions for such an effective, radical but hostile rule of law response by the ruling parties in 2015-23 to the above discontent.[3] In the doctrine, *Agnieszka Sadecka* distinguishes five types of this "discontent" underpinning populist governments.

These include historical discontent, perceived as a historical injustice affecting the whole nation, the injustice of the Yalta Agreement; a new politics of history, a "politics of remembrance", changes in curricula or "rewriting history" and the eternal struggle against communism are in response; the sense of betrayal by the West after the Second World War in turn gives rise to a permanent distrust of the West as such and Euroscepticism. The populists respond with anti-capitalist promises of a "real" welfare state, symbolized in Poland by the significance for many families of the "500 zloty-plus" family allowance. Important were also visions of the promised "repolonisation of the economy", albeit without nationalization of national assets by law, lowering of the retirement age or additional pensions.[4] The basic issue, however, remains to distinguish three less frequently discussed types of dissatisfaction as a cultural context. These types, with appropriate commentary from an administrative and legal point of view, should be spoken of more closely.

I. Ontological dissatisfaction

At the core of this narrative are a sense of meaninglessness and anxiety caused by accelerated change, very characteristic of postmodern culture.[5] The feeling of isolation in an already individualistic society reinforces the lack of control and agency, of being rooted. This leads to an expectation of something big, unifying, which will happen and which will engage "hearts and minds", or the arrival of someone, who will solve "with a strong hand" existing problems as *J. Kubik* states. The populist response to this anxiety and discontent is brought by the respective parties. Here is the following narrative of the report, partly supplemented by the comments of this paper:

---

mans czy dysonans. Raport Fundacji Stefana Batorego "Badania nad populizmem w Europie Środkowo-Wschodniej", 2022, p. 5 ff.

3 *Kubik*, *The* POPREBEL *and FATIGUE Manifesto*, 2018, available at: https://populism-europe.com/wp-content/uploads/2020/09/Working-Paper-1. (last access: 23.10.2025).

4 *Kubik* (fn. 3).

5 *Michalski* (ed.), Tożsamość w czasach zmiany. Rozmowy w Castel Gandolfo, 1995, p. 14 ff.

- a new model of collective identity, a community – no longer civic, but based on so-called "traditional values", national, ethnic and religious homogeneity;
- a new meaning of national symbols, myths and heroes, celebrated in a "turbo patriotic" way;[6]
- emphasis on the importance of religion in the state; a kind of political theology;
- traditional values concerning family life, celebrated in public as a myth and a political ideal, it should be added – often exposed by politicians who do not exemplify these values;
- a rhetoric of "state security and stability" that rejects subjects defined in terms of "aliens": immigrants, any minority.

All these elements have occurred in Polish conditions, whereby the excessive involvement of the Catholic church in political life, public religious celebrations with the participation of state officials, the violation of the constitutional "friendly separation" of church and state has paradoxically caused a significant decrease in religious practices. Public opinion polls emphasize the lack of acceptance for such – too close in their opinion – liaison between the state and the dominant Catholic Church in Poland, which – unlike in the tradition of the Orthodox Church – should, according to the majority of the population, be characterized by a healthy distance and the possibility for churches and religious groups to speak critically not only about social issues but generally about the state policy.

II. Cultural dissatisfaction

It is related to identity and consists of the following: the search for the aforementioned homogeneity, a high fear of cultural differences and of the blurring of identity and of external threats, attacks on and discrimination against various minority groups.[7]

---

6 *Napiórkowski*, Turbopatriotyzm, 2019, p. 6 ff.

7 *Bokszański*, Tożsamości zbiorowe, 2005, p. 70 ff., see there the role of the regions.

Populist responses include:

- nativism, anti-immigrant rhetoric, homogeneity;
- legal "protection" against the cultural threat caused by Europeanisation and/or globalisation;[8]
- celebrating what is "our own" as opposed to what is external and therefore foreign, for example in publicly funded media.
  The theses of the Batory Foundation's report should be supplemented at this point by emerging conspiracy theories – especially by disinformation and cognitive warfare portals – about the desire for a "cultural exchange" by hidden, hostile forces, together with the allegedly planned "swapping" of the entire "ruling class" of society. The feeling of absolute superiority associated with the dominant culture in a given country and the call for the complete adaptation to it of "foreigners" whose culture is despised, this applies even to those cultures, which are geographically close and not very different, according to the principle of the "fetishism of small differences", best illustrated by the wars in the former Yugoslavia and now by Russia's war against Ukraine.[9]
- Dissatisfaction with the state.

This narrative accentuates the lack of trust in state institutions, emphasizes the lack of agency, the helplessness of individuals in their relations with public institutions, criticizes the privatization of public services, which is best reflected in the notion created in the media of the "cardboard state".

The sense of individual oppression by the police, the justice system and even social welfare institutions is officially fueled and framed with isolated – but exposed even on billboards – negative examples of, for example, misguided administrative decisions and judgements and corrupt judges. The private lives of these individuals, using illegally obtained (*Pegasus* system) personal data of a sensitive nature, were then used for defamatory media campaigns in the public and private media.

It proved unexpectedly easy to undermine in the public consciousness the sense of the long, difficult, and much-sacrificed path of transformation towards freedom for the construction of a democratic state under the rule

---

8 *Ziółkowska*, Czy Europejczyk ma szansę stać się obywatelem Europy? Problem europejskiej tożsamości i postnarodowego obywatelstwa, in: Markiewicz/Wojnicki (eds.), Kryzys tożsamości politycznej a proces integracji europejskiej, 2006, p. 131.

9 *Etkind*, Rosja kontra nowoczesność, Warszawa 2024, p. 87 ff.

of law.[10] For after 30 years of transformation, it has already become clear to many families that they are now already permanently belonging to a lower social class with no prospect of lasting change, for example by their children obtaining higher education and the associated better paid jobs.

The populist response (not only according to the Batory Foundation report) includes the following points:

- the promise of "good change" in various areas of politics and social life through personnel purges and "new cadres" of populist parties coming from less favored individuals and families or those who have failed in their careers. Their allegiance and willingness to overstep the legal boundaries is far greater than that of people with a high sense of values and a large social capital;
- anti-elitism and an ever-publicized anti-corruption campaign, with symbolically always perpetrators from the elite, – but ignoring and even institutionally supporting nepotism;
- the reform of the judiciary – stringency and speed placed above human rights, ignoring the Constitution, laws and their procedures, – "the law of spectacle" according to *Ewa Łętowska's*[11] term;
- rhetoric portraying the central state always as a defender of the individual (the state as synonymous with the nation), while local self-government as "suspect" structures requiring strict supervision and restriction of their activities.

An additional element, closely related to the Polish specificity and an attempt to satisfy the "dissatisfaction with the State" was the drive towards recentralization and the taking away of tasks and competences from the local government, and in this respect, tasks that still remained the responsibility of the local government.[12] A decisive reduction in their financing was taking place in a manner contrary to the Constitution and the law.

10 *Stelmach,* Sztuka manipulacji, 2018, p. 53 ff.

11 *Łętowska,* Multicentryczność współczesnego systemu prawa i jej konsekwencje, Państwo i Prawo (PiP) 2005 no. 5, 4 (4 ff.).

12 *Korczak,* Wyzwania stojące przed samorządem terytorialnym (System..oop.cit. t. s. 768-769) comp. Calender of the recentralisation, in: *Sześciło, Przedańska, Szwast, Jakubek-Lalik, Kłucińska, Jakubowski,* Demokracja samorządna w: *Sześciło.* Polska samorządów. Silna demokracja, skuteczne państwo. Fundacja Batorego Warszawa 2019, p. 124 (125).

This was especially true, as *Sebastian Sikorski* pointed out[13], for health care tasks and the running of hospitals, in respect of which the illegal withholding of their funding was found in 2016, even by the Constitutional Court, which is friendly to those in power. It should also be stressed that the constant underfunding of the tasks of local government also made deep political sense: local government, unable to fulfil its tasks and competences, risked incurring the wrath of the local community, which could translate into a general turning away of sympathy from local government and putting all hopes in the leader of the state and his party. Local self-government had, in fact, due to its separate electoral rhythm, a number of units governed by the then opposition against the coalition of the *Law and Justice* and *Solidarna Polska* parties; it could therefore not be considered a reliable ally. A temporary solution for those in power under populist conditions seemed to be to favor politically close local government authorities and their units.

Territorial self-government was seen as the main opponent of public authority and, in addition to limiting its own tasks and funding, a kind of "symbolic violence" was deliberately introduced under the guise of belated decommunization, i.e. interference in such spheres as the names of streets and squares and monuments, in which the identity of the community was manifested, and decisions were taken by democratically elected commune and district councils and voivodship assemblies.

C. Digitalization as a driving force for the authoritarian backlash

According to the Polish doctrine, one of the reasons for these unfavorable changes was the delay in the transition from the stage of building a democratic state under the rule of law to the actual social state envisaged in the Constitution, despite its declarations about a social market economy. A hitherto patiently waiting society, building a "capitalism without capitalists" (but with the help of trade unions) deferred its individual ambitions and life plans for a long time. When it became apparent that the prospect of realizing their European Dream of prosperity was receding into the distance, they turned to other political groupings, which, in addition, through the use of the latest digital techniques, in particular the management-manipulation of algorithms in the style of *Cambridge Analytica*, have greatly increased the effectiveness of their management of the electorate. In the second term,

13 *Sikorski*, Administracja ochrony zdrowia, 2021, p. 8-12.

however, there was, as the State Electoral Commission pointed out, an abuse of public funds for party purposes in the election campaign.

A coherent, professionally crafted political narrative about the superfluousness, meaninglessness of long-term sacrifices, humiliation and stigmatization of "simple people" made politics appealing to the emotions again. Even the name of the party "*Law and Justice*" fits into the trend of "romantic" populist party names like "Georgian Dream", which was a manifestation of the takeover of the mainstream social narrative. Public destruction also brought popularity.

The destruction of authority undermines the foundations of democracy, but also points to a long-standing deficit in co-optation processes and social communication with patients, petitioners or customers. In this respect, too, digitalization and the reality of the web have played a great role. The sense of apparent omnipotence and omniscience provided by global search engines has transformed the interaction with those exercising public authority. Patients commonly come with their own diagnosis, armed sometimes even with hundreds of specialized information from the web. The same applies to petitioners or students. Never before has it been so easy to question authority, e.g. due to ignorance of details achievable to the layman on the web. As *Maria Ossowska* pointed out, democracy badly needs its personal role models, so their destruction is particularly dangerous.[14]

D. The impact of the authoritarian backlash on the institutions

Why, then, in spite of political success and a long period in power, including the complete, albeit illegal, mastery of the public media and their transformation into entities with a dominant pro-government narrative, as well as mass propaganda of success, was populism – it is not known whether finally – pushed out of power in the last elections in Poland – despite a large number of votes? Does this represent a break in the trend and an element of hope for other European countries? Have state actors managed, thanks to institutional legal safeguards, to survive a period of populist offensive and to preserve their independence?

A huge surprise in the period of the destruction of the democratic state of law was the extremely rapid and effective "hollowing out" of the basic institutions of democratic representation, i.e. the *Sejm* (the lower chamber

14 *Ossowska*, Wzór demokraty, 1992, p. 7 ff.

of parliament) – in the sense of a total blockade of all initiatives of the opposition and normal parliamentary cooperation and other direct and indirect subjects of administration and control; the retention by the opposition of power over the Senate was a certain slowdown of change, but – due to the limited competences of the Senate in the Polish political system – it was a slowdown rather than an obstacle to reaching full power. This also applied to the Supreme Court and the Constitutional Tribunal; the Supreme Administrative Court resisted destructive actions for a relatively long time.

The rapid pace of these changes has been discussed in Polish literature by *Jerzy Stępień*.[15] He stressed that the first amendment to the Constitutional Court Act took place on 19 November 2015, and in the following weeks, the Parliament, quickly passed a number of laws of fundamental importance to the rule of law, including two new amendments to the Constitutional Court Act, an amendment to the Broadcasting Act, amendments to the Police Act and the Civil Service Act. The set of radical laws was closed by the new Law on the Public Prosecutor's Office (Law of 28 January 2016[16]), of which Article 137 § 2. reads: "*It does not constitute a disciplinary offence for a prosecutor to act or omit to act solely in the public interest.*" [translation by the author].[17]

The amendment to the Civil Service Act put an end to an impartial, reliable and politically neutral civil service, leaving its remains at lower levels. This came about through the abolition of competitions for senior government positions, allowing people to be employed in top ministerial positions on a party-appointed basis.

The staffing of positions in the public electronic media was placed in the hands of the Minister of the Treasury, the police were given wider scope for telephone tapping without prior court approval, and the heavily hierarchical prosecution service was fully subordinated to the Minister of Justice. This sequence of rapid legal changes led to destruction in key areas of the tri-partite government.

---

15 *Stępień*, Rewolucja – świadoma czy nieświadoma? Ruch Prawniczy, Ekonomiczny i Socjologiczny (RPEiS), 2016 no. 1, 19 (19 ff.).

16 Dz. U. 2016, poz. 177.

17 *Gerecka-Żołyńska*, Niezależność prokuratury i prokuratorów – nowe rozwiązania na tle dotychczasowych kontrowersji (uwagi w związku z ustawą z 28 stycznia 2016 r. – Prawo o prokuraturze), Ruch Prawniczy, Ekonomiczny I Socjologiczny (RPEiS) 78(1), 57 (57 ff.).

As *Jerzy Stępień* emphatically stated, "*The institutions of the rule of law function as long as they are respected by those in power.*"[18] The moment they place themselves above the law, the rule of law is only an unrealizable idea, and the law, or rather legislation, becomes merely an instrument for implementing the will of those in power – pure power in action, which, at any time, can dictate the rules of the game, and further: "*The rule of law does not consist in the arbitrary enactment of laws and other legal provisions – even in states respecting the rule of law there are excesses of those in power in breaking the law. The modern democratic state under the rule of law is democracy*". It should also be emphasized, that "*between 19 November and 12 February 2016, the parliament adopted 35 bills without any amendments from the Senate out of the 45 bills passed during that period.*" This was an unprecedented situation in over 25 years of free democratic political transformation, indicating the destruction of legislative power.[19]

Due to the complicated procedure for the appointment of the body, it turned out, unexpectedly, that a high resistance to manipulation was demonstrated by the office of the Ombudsman (*Ombudsman*) which, due to the mode of election with the participation of the Senate and with its consent, managed to maintain its independence throughout the period of the rule of the United Right, and its new election after five attempts had to take place in a mode of compromise with the opposition. However, the functioning of this body under the blockade of the Constitutional Court was extremely difficult.[20]

As a result of a series of political conflicts, the Supreme Audit Office (*NIK*) also retained its unexpected independence; its provision of objective documentation for most of its term of office, despite the partial personnel blockade of the *NIK* Collegium, was of great importance for the objectivity of the conflict.

However, this was an exception; the other bodies were reappointed effectively, even if in an unlawful manner. So-called "duplicate" judges were elected, and duly elected judges of the Constitutional Tribunal were not sworn in by the President of the State, making it impossible for them to take

18 *Stępień* (fn. 15), p. 29.

19 *Stępień* (fn. 15), p. 29 note 19.

20 More about this issue *Lipowicz*, Ombudsmann in Polen, Verteidiger der Rechte und Freiheiten in Krisenzeiten, in: *Hofmann/Höhlscheidt/Mörth/Pirker/Pöschl/Wiederin* (eds.), Festschrift für Franz Merli, 2023, p. 267 f. See also *Zoll*, Sposób wyboru sędziów Trybunału Konstytucyjnego, 2016, Ruch Prawniczy, Ekonomiczny I Socjologiczny (RPEiS) 78(1), 43 (43-50).

up their duties under the new Civil Service Act, leading to a fundamental erosion of the civil service in the unanimous opinion of doctrine.[21]

While, due to its anchoring in the Constitution, the highest levels of the civil service were still formally maintained, the rest was already staffed according to political criteria on a spoils basis and in a way that was very reminiscent of the principle of party nomenclature known from the previous regime. Impartiality, professionalism, competitive appointments, transparent action, and the cross-party nature of the civil service were all nullified. This meant, however, that far-reaching changes could be made to thousands of officials.

E. Local resistance

With all the breadth of these changes, the structure of local self-government was not finally destroyed. For 8 years, successive tasks and competences were taken away from the self-government, in contravention of the principle of subsidiarity, which is also a constitutional principle in Poland, and in contravention of the order to decentralize directly enshrined in the Constitution. Despite this, social loyalty to such limited self-government was not broken; thus, one may speculate that belonging to a community, being rooted in it, a sense of participation and influence on local and supra-local matters partially weakened the attractiveness of the "populist response" characterized at the outset. The loneliness of the isolated individual, so typical of authoritarian and totalitarian countries, was not achieved.

The original structure of local government created in 1990/1998 was strong. However, can we measure the success of the survival of local government despite extremely unfavorable boundary conditions? There are two important elements here: firstly, a high degree of public confidence in local government (around 70% in subsequent surveys and beyond), a confidence which exceeds that of the central government many times over; secondly, the repeated terms of office of directly elected local government executive bodies. The permanence of once established local elites has of course complex causes and is also slowly becoming a cause for concern and

21 *Ura*, Pracownicy samorządowi, in: Lipowicz (ed.), System Prawa Samorządowego Vol. 2, 2022, p. 947 ff.

planned adjustment of the local government system, but it does strengthen the sense of confidence and rootedness in the local government.[22]

Another element is the high level of activity in social consultations and, in particular, the development of the institution of the civic budget, i.e. proactivity and innovation. Local self-government in Poland is of course not ideal; nepotism and the lack of a self-governing civilian corps remain serious problems, but it was characteristic that local self-government units courageously and independently became involved in helping Ukrainian refugees in 2022, but also illegal immigrants at the Polish-Belarusian border, explicitly against official government policy with anti-immigrant features.

Despite the fact that the government administration "rewarded and punished" pro-government behavior by, for example, differentiating road fund subsidies, as demonstrated by *Swianiewicz's* research, local authorities were confident enough in them after all truncated independence to have the courage to take similar action.[23] The announced abolition of districts, on the other hand, was hampered by a political barrier – many members of the United Right were also active in this local government.

Despite the problems and attempts to centralize their own tasks, Poland's local government remained a major source of innovation; its flexibility and dynamism contrast sharply with the archaic and rigid structure and functioning of the government administration, unreformed for years and plagued by departmental divisions.[24]

F. What needs to be done

The central administration most strongly associated with the government after 8 years, in the view of most voters, has failed to deliver on its populist promises. The inability to manage the Covid-19 pandemic crisis and the dysfunctions of areas in this administration that have not been reformed for years: post office, railways, health care, fiscal administration not sufficiently

22 *Korczak*, Wyzwania stojące przed samorządem terytorialnym, in: Lipowicz (ed.), System prawa samorządu terytorialnego Vol. 3, 2023, p. 743 f. and p. 775 ff.

23 *Swianiewicz*, Raport Fundacji Batorego w kwestii Funduszu Drogowego. „Najwyższa Izba kontroli o Funduszu Dróg samorządowych", ed. NIK Warszawa, 12 August 2021.

24 *Korczak*, Decentralizacja i recentralizacja w administracji publicznej na przykładzie zadań własnych i zleconych jednostek samorządu terytorialnego, in: Ura/Pieprzny (eds.), Aktualne problemy funkcjonowania samorządu, 2017, p. 17 and p. 25.

pursuing the goals of fighting inflation got through to the public through daily experience, despite the dominant government coverage in the public media.

In addition to the tightening of abortion laws, it was high inflation and the inefficiency of meeting collective needs at the central level, including the misguided reform of the judiciary generating only further conflicts, that contributed to the change of government. Populist promises of simple solutions in government and the economy are disappointing after a few years; however, this is a race against time, as the simultaneous control of political and state structures means that democratic change – even as a result of the widespread disillusionment of many voters – may already prove to be almost impossible, as in Hungary.

It is the reform of the central administration that seems most important in Poland at the moment – already with the authorities back in power. After all, the position of the central administration has been eroded by European law on the one hand, and increasingly mature local government and active non-governmental organizations exercising outsourced administration on the other. This requires a new approach to achieving a resilient, lightweight and flexible networked administration. However, one with clear structures of responsibility within the office; such an administration could make, along with the other elements discussed above, another populist response to discontent with the state and cultural dissatisfaction unnecessary.

The focus of central administration should not be on reducing the tasks and competences of local government, but on sound oversight which does not exclude the autonomy of these units. The new central administration should be crisis-proof, but also actively defend the institutions of a democratic state under the rule of law and – like local government – be equipped with a range of new functions, for example an expanded, modern civil defence.

Since the last reform of the central administration in Poland, there has also been a profound digital transformation and this requires the greatest consideration in structures and procedures.[25] It seems that serious reform and funding is also required for the administration of culture, which is becoming increasingly important, since a large part of the populist response

25 *Szafrański*, Realizacja zadań publicznych a Big data, in: Szpor (ed.), Publiczne bazy danych i internet Warszawa, 2014, p. 4 f.; *Szpor*, Transformacja cyfrowa, in: Lipowicz (ed.), System Prawa Samorządu terytorialnego Vol. 3, 2023, p. 624 and p. 635.

to ontological and cultural discontent is concentrated in the area of identity, culture; here too there is much to be done.

General regional education strengthens the sense of identity, but within the framework of a democratic state of law it is so far only practiced in a few regions in Poland; extending it to the whole of Poland would make it possible to have an informed conversation about discrimination, exclusion of minorities, traditions without populism.

Up to now the typical work of political education and preparation for democracy has been financed by European funds to a much lesser extent than infrastructure; meanwhile it is already known that the turning away of the communities of the member states from the European idea, even if, as in the case of Brexit, many will later regret it, turns out to be crucial for the survival of the European Union. Democracy costs money, and so does the rule of law; it is in the common interest of Europeans to allocate more funds in the next budget perspective to consolidate the fundamental values of the European Union, without which democracy and the rule of law will not survive in Europe, and to strengthen local self-government, which is a kind of "rescue for Europe", effective, as the Polish example shows, also in longer, difficult periods of populism.

Valid and invalid national identity claims under Article 4(2) TEU and the ECJ's role

Kriszta Kovács[*]

A. Introduction

Europe is a "*community of law*" that "*puts the rule of law in the place of power and its manipulation*" and "*replaces violence and political pressure*"[1] – said *Walter Hallstein* in the 1950s. He was a driving force behind the construction of the European Community and then the Union. For *Hallstein*, the concept of a union based on shared values agreed upon in law was a concept deeply embedded in an attempt to learn from the violent history of the 1930s and 1940s in Europe. If this is accurate, what happens when the rule of law is destroyed is obvious. Should the law fail, power and manipulation will prevail once again. So, when the rule of law is attacked and dismantled in an EU Member State today, this is what is at stake.

The attacks on fundamental principles of constitutionalism, such as the protection of fundamental rights or the rule of law, come in a variety of ways that destroy the fabric of democracy. There has been a forceful resurgence of anti-Semitism, Islamophobia and ethnonationalist racism,[2] and this has been orchestrated, inspired, or tolerated by governments once constitutionalism is gone. Judicial systems, right next to independent media

* This paper draws on the introduction and the chapter I co-authored with *Susanne Baer* and *Maya Vogel*. See *Baer/Kovács/Vogel*, Constitutionalism Today: The Prospects of the European Constitutional Community, in: Kovács (ed.), The Jurisprudence of Particularism. National Identity Claims in Central Europe, 2023, p. 187 (193). An earlier version of this piece was given at the 2024 Hallstein-Colloquium of the *Merton-Centre* at Goethe University in Frankfurt am Main on 21/22 March 2024. Thanks to the participants at this workshop, especially to Prof. *Stefan Kadelbach* and Prof. *Rainer Hofmann* for their useful comments and feedback. I am grateful to *Julian Leonhard* for research assistance. But of course, responsibility for the content lies solely with me.

1 *Hallstein*, Europe in the Making, 1972, p. 30 ff.

2 *Braunschweiger/Teffera/Wilkes*, Interview: Antisemitism and Islamophobia Spike in Europe, 18.12.2023, available at https://www.hrw.org/news/2023/12/18/interview-antisemitism-and-islamophobia-spike-europe (last access: 5 Jan 2026).

and education, have been dismantled rather quickly in some places.[3] There seems to be a recipe for mixing these ingredients into a toxic dish: They serve populism, crude essentialist nationalism, and contempt for democratic institutions, including courts.

The characteristic I focus on in this piece is casting a "constitutional", or in effect, a "national identity" as a limit to European integration. In an ideal world, there would be very little space for the terms "constitutional identity" or "national identity" in the legal domain. This is because the term "identity" is loaded and vague and lacks the necessary precision to serve as a legal concept.[4] And even in our non-ideal world, these terms did not play any role in European legal discourse for a long time. In the past, other concepts resolved the problem of allocation of competencies within the European Union. For instance, the concept of sovereignty long framed the discourse: courts interpreted democracy through the lens of the sovereign state and used the concept of sovereignty to draw boundaries to European integration.[5]

In the 2000s, a conceptual shift happened: the relevance of the concept of sovereignty declined, and the concepts of constitutional and national identity became part of the continent's legal repertoire.[6] The German Federal Constitutional Court (*Bundesverfassungsgericht*), the French Constitutional Court (*Conseil constitutionnel)* and the Spanish Constitutional Tribunal (*Tribunal constitucional)* started to use the language of "constitutional identity"[7] to draw certain red lines relating to further European integration. Since then, other European constitutional courts have embedded the language of identity in their own jurisprudence.[8]

3 *Kovács/Scheppele*, The fragility of an independent judiciary: Lessons from Hungary and Poland—and the European Union, Communist & Post-Communist Stud. 51 (2018), 189.

4 As *Brubaker* and *Cooper* put it, identity "*tends to mean too much (when understood in a strong sense), too little (when understood in a weak sense), or nothing at all (because of its sheer ambiguity)*", cf. *Brubaker/Cooper*, Beyond "identity", Theory & Society 29 (2000), 1.

5 *Toniatti*, Sovereignty Lost, Constitutional Identity Regained, in: Arnaiz/Llivina (eds.), National Constitutional Identity and European Integration, 2013, p. 49 (54).

6 *Weiler*, On the power of the Word: Europe's constitutional iconography, I.CON 3 (2005), 173 (184).

7 *Claes*, National Identity: Trump Card or Up for Negotiation?, in: Arnaiz/Llivina (eds.), National Constitutional Identity and European Integration, 2013, p. 109 (124).

8 *Faraguna*, Taking Constitutional Identities away from the Courts, Brook J. Int'l L. 41 (2015), 491 (492).

B. The Concepts of Constitutional and National Identity in Positive Law

Currently, both the concepts of constitutional identity and national identity play a central role as a matter of positive law. Constitutional identity case law has prominence in European constitutional jurisprudence. Its function is to give justifications for the Member States not to obey the primacy of EU law as demanded by the Court of Justice of the European Union (ECJ)[9] by drawing boundaries to the implementation of EU law. The concept of national identity is also present in the European legal space. The Lisbon Treaty[10], which amended the two treaties that form the European Union's constitutional basis, introduced "national identity" as a justiciable concept to challenge the domestic courts' interpretation. The concept's importance was emphasised by the fact that it was reproduced in the preamble of the EU Fundamental Rights Charter.[11] Today, Art. 4(2) of the Treaty on European Union (TEU) obliges the European Union to respect the national identities of the Member States. Although EU law explicitly uses the notion of "national identity", Art. 4(2) contextually suggests that national identity has a constitutional relevance.[12] Hence, although EU law refers to national identity, its concept is essentially constitutionalist.

Yet, not every Member State applies the term "national identity" in this constitutional sense. There are problematic applications of the concept. What are these problematic applications? In the early 21st century, a global backlash developed against universal, integrative constitutional principles: human rights, democracy and the rule of law. National identity was rediscovered in common ancestry and shared ethnocultural heritage, which enabled governments to advance exclusivist constitutional agendas. This phenomenon is not limited to the Central European region, so it may not be explained away by references to the unique characteristics of post-socialist states, with their long history of authoritarianism and limited experience of democracy. However, this region has recently exhibited the most visible signs of exclusionary nationalism in the European Union.

9 The Court of Justice of the European Union comprises two separate courts: The Court of Justice (the higher instance) and the General Court (the lower instance). The higher instance is abbreviated as ECJ.

10 Treaty of Lisbon – Amending the Treaty on European Union and the Treaty Establishing The European Community, O.J. C 306/1.

11 Charter of Fundamental Rights of the European Union, Preamble, 2012/C 326/02.

12 *Toniatti* (fn. 5), p. 63.

Exclusionary nationalism is not new. What is novel is that these countries have cited Art. 4(2) TEU as grounds for limiting the authority of EU law. In 2015, Hungary and Slovakia claimed that the European Union should accommodate their distinctive national identities that are based on the rejection of migration and multiculturalism and allow them to refrain from participating in the EU refugee relocation scheme.[13] In a similar vein, the Bulgarian, Hungarian, Polish and Slovak governments argued in 2020 that the so-called "*'traditional' family*" is a value protected as an element of national identity in EU law, so the European Union should allow these countries to avoid recognising same-sex marriage.[14] Later, Poland invoked the national identity reservation of Art. 4(2) TEU when it "reorganised" the Polish court jurisdiction and introduced special chambers such as the disciplinary chamber.[15]

Interestingly, when using the "identity language", these governments and the apex courts of these countries frequently refer to the case law of the German Federal Constitutional Court.[16] This reference to the German identity review as a shield against supranational law is not a coincidence. The Federal Constitutional Court often bases its identity decisions on an idiosyncratic "German" understanding of democracy,[17] which risks becoming a kind of self-centred constitutional identity jurisprudence, where the domestic actors are the only ones deemed competent to contribute.[18] This interpretation provides reference points for the Central European constitu-

13 This political claim transformed into legal claims in the joined cases ECJ, *Slovak Republic and Hungary (supported by the Republic of Poland) v. Council of the European Union,* C-643/15 and C-647/15, ECLI:EU:C:2017:631.

14 The Hungarian, Polish and Slovak governments submitted written observations on the issue arguing for the 'traditional' family model in the case ECJ, *VMA v. Stolichna obshtina, rayon 'Pancharevo'* (Sofia municipality, Pancharevo district, Bulgaria), C-490/20, ECLI:EU:C:2021:1008. See the Opinion of Advocate General *Kokott* delivered on 15 April 2021, ECLI:EU:C:2021:296, paras 30, 69 ff.

15 See ECJ, *European Commission v. Republic of Poland,* C-204/21, ECLI:EU:C:2023:442.

16 *Rideau,* The Case-law of the Polish, Hungarian and Czech Constitutional Courts on National Identity and the 'German Model', in: Arnaiz/Llivina (eds.), National Constitutional Identity and European Integration, 2013, p. 243 (250). *Komárek,* Czech Constitutional Court Playing with Matches: The Czech Constitutional Court Declares a Judgment of the Court of Justice of the EU Ultra Vires; Judgment of 31 January 2012, Pl. ÚS 5/12, Slovak Pensions XVII, Eu Const. L. Rev. 8 (2012), 323.

17 *Halberstam/Möllers,* The German Constitutional Court Says 'Ja Zu Deutschland!', GLJ 10 (2009), 1241 (1258).

18 *Çali,* The Two Faces of German Legal Hegemony?, 7.10.2020, available at: https://verfassungsblog.de/the-two-faces-german-legal-hegemony/ (last access: 5 Jan 2026).

tional courts. Nevertheless, the essence, content and aim of identity review in Germany are different from the jurisprudence of many Central European apex courts.

C. Varied Judicial Understandings of Identity

In German constitutional jurisprudence, the Federal Constitutional Court has developed the doctrine of constitutional identity to protect the core values of the German Basic Law (*Grundgesetz*).[19] It is based on the explicit "eternity clause" (*Ewigkeitsgarantie*) in Art. 79(3) of the German Basic Law, which does not allow for any constitutional amendment ever to change the core content of the constitution. The Federal Constitutional Court called this constitutional identity, or "*Verfassungsidentität*"[20], and held that neither domestic law nor any international agreement or institutional arrangement could change this core content.[21] The concept of constitutional identity as developed by the Federal Constitutional Court is understood in a politico-constitutional sense; hence, it is an integrative mirror identity in which all members of the society may recognise themselves. Moreover, the constitutional identity in Germany is qualified by the requirement of Europe-friendliness.[22] The Federal Constitutional Court takes into account Germany's commitments to ensure the success of European integration, gives due regard to EU law supremacy in general, and only claims the need to intervene when the Basic Law would require more baseline protection of fundamental rights[23] and more democratic accountability[24] than EU

19 In addition to the identity control, the Court also checks whether institutions whose competences have been handed to them by the state do indeed act within such limitations or "ultra vires" and whether EU measures respect fundamental rights.

20 More on this, see *Polzin*, Identity and Eternity: The German Concept of Constitutional Identity, in: Kovács (ed.), The Jurisprudence of Particularism. National Identity Claims in Central Europe, 2023, p. 58.

21 BVerfGE 113, 273 (*European Arrest Warrant I*); BVerfGE 123, 267 (*Lisbon*); BVerfGE 126, 286 (*Honeywell*); BVerfGE 129, 78 (*Cassina*); BVerfGE 134, 366 (*OMT*); BVerfGE 140, 317 (*European Arrest Warrant II*). The Federal Constitutional Court has not deemed it violated to date.

22 See the *Lisbon* judgment of the German Federal Constitutional Court BVerfGE 123, 267 (357).

23 BVerfGE 73, 339 (*Solange II*); BVerfGE 152, 152 (*Right to be Forgotten I*); BVerfGE 152, 216 (*Right to be Forgotten II*).

24 For instance, by demanding enhanced justifications from the European Central Bank in the so called *PSPP* decision, see BVerfGE 154, 17.

law. The goal is thus better protection of human rights and democratic principles within the European Union and the creation of a culture of constitutional obedience.[25]

A formally doctrinal concept of constitutional identity such as the one developed by the German Federal Constitutional Court can, in principle, be fully compatible with the commitment to European values in Art. 2 TEU, especially if the domestic apex court emphasises European commonalities and not the differences in its rulings on the main treaties and on fundamental rights.

In this spirit, the Federal Constitutional Court issued several "warnings" to European institutions. It called on European institutions to live up to the common constitutional commitments based on treaty law: the principle of democracy (Art. 2 TEU and Art. 20 of the German Basic Law) and the rule of law (also in Art. 2 TEU and Art. 20 of the German Basic Law). These "warnings" corresponded to Art. 23 of the German Basic Law, which obliges German state institutions to participate in and facilitate the integration process.[26]

By contrast, several constitutional courts in Central Europe have used the concepts of constitutional identity and national identity to establish limits on European integration and lower the level of domestic protection of human rights. Moreover, the captured institutions still called constitutional courts, such as the Hungarian Constitutional Court and the Polish Constitutional Tribunal,[27] have applied a hollow copy of the concept of constitutional identity by filling it with the nation's (ethno)cultural charac-

---

25 *Alter*, National Perspectives on International Constitutional Review: Diverging Optics, in: Delaney/Dixon (eds.), Comparative Judicial Review, 2018, p. 244 ff.

26 In the 1970s, the famous *Solange I* and *II* decisions of the German Federal Constitutional Court emphasized that ECJ rulings would be accepted "*as long as*" [translation by the author] (in German: *solange*) they conformed to the protection of fundamental rights, at a time when there was no such Charter (BVerfGE 37, 271; BVerfGE 73, 339). Yet it is important that there was no divergence of basic values but a debate over what would best realise these values in a given case. More on this see the special issue of the Heidelberg Journal of International Law (ZaöRV) 'Solange 50th Anniversary: Constitutionalism Beyond the State and the Role of Domestic Constitutional Courts', ZaöRV 85 (2025), 399. The Right to be Forgotten rulings gave rise to a "dialogue" between the EU Charter, the European Convention on Human Rights, and the German Basic Law, see BVerfGE 152, 152 and BVerfGE 152, 216.

27 According to the European Court of Human Rights, the current Polish Constitutional Tribunal is not a lawfully established independent and impartial tribunal. ECHR, *Xero Flor w Polsce sp. Z o.o. v. Poland* (7.5.2021), App. no. 4907/18.

teristics. This leads down a path of dismissing EU law and ECJ rulings on the grounds of (ethno)nationalistic ideology.[28]

D. An Example: Human Dignity as an Element of Constitutional Identity

To take an example, constitutional identity is often shaped by the judicial interpretation of human dignity. The origins of the principle of human dignity can be traced to the idea of our presumptive shared humanity and to the fact that political communities like states or the EU are committed to this constitutional principle. EU law in general and the Lisbon Treaty in particular confirm and endorse the fundamental significance of the principle of human dignity. Yet, under the assumption that Member States uphold constitutional democracy and are devoted to this principle, EU law leaves it to the national apex courts to contextualise and interpret the concept of human dignity within their domestic legal systems.

In Germany, constitutional identity encompasses the concept of human dignity. Art. 1(1) of the German Basic Law starts by declaring that "*Human dignity shall be inviolable.*" [official translation by the *Sprachendienst des Deutschen Bundestages*]. It then obliges all state authority to respect and protect human dignity. This universalist obligation played a crucial role in the judgment of the German Federal Constitutional Court, which concerned the legal provisions governing basic cash benefits provided for in the Asylum Seekers Benefits Act. The Court was asked to determine whether the cash benefits paid under this Act were sufficient to ensure a minimum standard of living for the recipient. The Court's response was negative, noting its evident inadequacy due to its lack of adjustment since 1993, and obliged state authorities to guarantee the protection of human dignity for all affected individuals. Thus, the Court upheld the universal nature of basic human rights by emphasising that "*human dignity, guaranteed in Art. 1(1) of the Basic Law, may not be modified in light of migration-policy considerations*"[29].

28 *Fabbrini/Sajó*, The Dangers of Constitutional Identity, ELJ 25 (2019), 457; *Halmai*, Abuse of Constitutional Identity. The Hungarian Constitutional Court on Interpretation of Article E) (2) of the Fundamental Law, Rev. Cent. & E. Eur. L. 43 (2018), 23; *Kovács*, The Rise of an Ethnocultural Constitutional Identity in the Jurisprudence of the East Central European Courts, GLJ 18 (2017), 1703.

29 BVerfGE 132, 134 (173) (*Asylum-Seekers' Benefits Act*) [official translation by the court].

Hungary's 1989 democratic constitution pledged to uphold the universal principle of human dignity and granted the courts a free hand in its interpretation.[30] By contrast, the current constitution, known as the Fundamental Law, asserts the importance of human dignity but with certain conditions[31] and ties it to Christianity. It also obliges the courts to interpret it based on the national identity outlined in an ethnocultural manner by the Fundamental Law.[32] Against this background, the captured Hungarian Constitutional Court created a right to "self-identity and self-determination" for people with "traditional social identities" living in Hungary, a "right" that, according to the decision, derives from the right to human dignity. The decision then declared that this "right" is violated "*if a foreign population remains permanently and en masse on the territory of Hungary without democratic authorisation*", and that the state is obliged to protect the Hungarians' "*right to self-identity*" from "*foreign populations*".[33] As a result, the universalist obligation to uphold the dignity of every person transformed into a particular privilege to safeguard ethnic Hungarians.

One reason for this difference in the judicial interpretation of constitutional identity might be that the captured Hungarian "Court" has not included the whole constitutional concept. It has tended to load the concept of identity with diffuse notions of (ethno)nationalism rather than applying it in accordance with universal constitutional principles. To counter such a trend, European institutions need to act, but how?

E. The Role of the ECJ: Differentiating Between Valid and Invalid Forms of National Identity Claims

National identity became justiciable in the European Union when the Lisbon Treaty came into force in 2009. Since then, domestic courts' inter-

30 Art. 54(1) of said constitution.

31 *Dupré*, Human Dignity: Rhetoric, Protection, and Instrumentalisation, in: Tóth (ed.), Constitution for a Disunited Nation: On Hungary's 2011 Fundamental Law, 2012, p. 143 (169).

32 The National Avowal part of the Fundamental Law suggests that "*Hungary's constitutional self-identity*" is distinctively and uniquely rooted in its "*historical constitution*", and in "*the Holy Crown, which embodies the state's constitutional continuity and nation's unity*". In addition, several articles connect "*Hungary's self-identity*" to "*Christian culture*". See, e.g., Art. R(4) and Art. XVI(1).

33 Decision 32/2021. (XII. 20.) AH határozat [translation by the author]. The captured Hungarian Constitutional Court is obliged to defend this "national identity" even against the ECJ.

pretations of national identity can be challenged before the ECJ. National identity claims by the EU Member States can take various forms. They can conform to universal constitutional principles, which occurs when domestic judges interpret and contextualise these principles in accordance with those very same principles. Yet not everything that a Member State presents as national identity pertains to its national identity as protected under Art. 4(2) TEU. There are national identity claims that are not consistent with the European community's underlying values: the protection of human rights, democracy and the rule of law.

How can the valid forms of national identity claims be distinguished from those that violate the EU Member States' constitutional commitments as outlined in Art. 2 TEU? First, let me look at what the current ECJ case law suggests, and then I will recommend how the ECJ can move forward to protect the EU values listed under Art. 2 TEU better.

There is a reason for the existence of Art. 4(2) TEU, which mandates EU institutions to respect the national identities of Member States. The EU, as *Walter Hallstein* rightly pointed out, operates as a "community of law"[34]. Art. 2 TEU establishes the fundamental legal principles, including democracy, the rule of law, and equality, among others, on which the EU is built. Yet, the abstract nature of these principles requires national institutions to provide context and interpretation within their domestic legal system. While a literal understanding of Art. 4(2) TEU may suggest that any domestic interpretation of national identity would be consistent with EU law, this provision does not give a blank cheque for the Member States to construct whatever national identity they may prefer at a given time.

Domestic constitutions and their interpretations may contain provisions that contradict fundamental principles of constitutionalism. Therefore, not

34 This "community of law" is safeguarded, among others, through the preliminary reference procedure in ensuring the consistency of EU law: If a provision of EU law is not clear to a domestic court, it can seek guidance from the ECJ, which will issue a ruling on the interpretation of the law that must be adhered to throughout the EU. Note that the Hungarian Act LXXXV of 2023 added a new constitutional court procedure to the 2011 Act on the Constitutional Court. In this "reverse preliminary ruling procedure", the Hungarian Constitutional Court, at the request of the ECJ, gives a preliminary opinion on the interpretation of Hungary's constitutional structure, order, requirements, traditions, national identity, sovereignty and its inalienable right to its population (Article 16/A of Act CLI of 2011 on the Constitutional Court). This amendment reflects a clear misconception about the function of the preliminary reference. While EU law mandates compliance from Member States, Hungarian laws do not apply to EU institutions.

all that a Member State claims as part of its national identity falls within the scope of protection under Art. 4(2) TEU. Certainly, there is space for cultural diversity, like the protection of national languages, provided that they are connected to the national constitutional identity embodied by the domestic legal system from the moment of the foundation of the independent and democratic state.[35] So, the ECJ case law features a conditional element, a substantive criterion tied to constitutionalist principles. Hence, even though Art. 4(2) TEU expressly refers to "national" identity, it actually pertains to a constitutional idea. As the ECJ puts it, the values on "*which the European Union is founded*" and which "*define the very identity of the European Union as a legal order common to those States*"[36] are the bases that have to be agreed on within all Member States. Consequently, the EU has an obligation to respect national identities as long as identity retention does not undermine the EU foundational principles ensured by Art. 2 TEU.[37]

Within the European Union, it is for the ECJ to decide whether a national identity claim is valid as a matter of EU law and can justify derogations from EU law.[38] During this judicial exercise, the ECJ does not define the national identity of a country; its role is solely to assess if the Member State's claim of national identity claim presented aligns with EU law. The ECJ has the option to define the term "national identity" in light of the prevailing constitutional structure of the Member State in question or treat the concept of "national identity" as autonomous.[39] The first assessment would require the ECJ to be utterly familiar with the twenty-seven different constitutional structures of the EU Member States.

---

35 *Kovács*, Constitutional or Ethnocultural? National Identity as a European Legal Concept, Intersections. East European Journal of Society and Politics 8 (2022), 170 (172).

36 ECJ, *Hungary v. Parliament and Council*, C-156/21, ECLI:EU:C:2022:97; and ECJ, *Poland v. Parliament and Council*, C-157/21, ECLI:EU:C:2022:98, para. 145.

37 *Konstadinides*, Constitutional Identity as a Shield and as a Sword: The European Legal Order within the Framework of national Constitutional Settlement, Camb. Yearb. Eur. Leg. Stud. 13 (2011), 195; *Sadurski*, Poland's Constitutional Breakdown, 2019, p. 223.

38 Although it flows from the ECJ's established case law, in the *VMA* case, Advocate General *Kokott* expressly stated that the ECJ is the gatekeeper of national identities, cf. *Kokott* (fn. 14), para. 70.

39 Advocate General *Kokott* suggests the ECJ to understand it as an autonomous concept of EU law cf. *Kokott* (fn. 14), para. 70.

Given the ECJ's role, it would thus be more fitting for it to characterise the concept of "national identity" as autonomous.[40] If the ECJ did offer an autonomous interpretation of "national identity", it would be able to control what national identity claims are acceptable. There are some indications in the case law that the ECJ is willing to adopt this approach. The ECJ pays respectful attention to domestic constitutional courts' interpretations and has proven to be sensitive to the definitions of constitutional identity as expressed by domestic judiciaries. However, domestic constitutions and their interpretations may contain anti-constitutional principles. This arises, for instance, when national identity claims are in large part informed by (ethno)cultural and historical myths. Hence, demonstrating national identity requires more than just inserting a particular provision into domestic constitutional law.

But how can legitimate and illegitimate national identity claims be distinguished? ECJ judgments suggest that in the ECJ's understanding, national identity is a legal phenomenon embodied in domestic law from the moment of the foundation of the independent and democratic state. This judicial approach is not very far from what I endorse in this piece.

F. A Possible Way Forward

The ECJ case law already encompasses the essential elements: first, that the concept of national identity is a legal concept and second, that this concept is connected to an independent and democratic state.

It is crucial from a constitutional point of view to limit the notion of identity to a strictly legal claim. Otherwise, those who see the European Union primarily as an economic organisation may transform their rejection of EU rights, principles and values into national identity claims. This is especially tempting for autocrats who use legalistic makeup to cover their authoritarian ways – they claim to be "simply following what others are doing", which is, in fact, an abuse of comparative constitutional law.

The ECJ has already made clear that the legal concept of national identity is connected to the independent and democratic state. Although the relevant ECJ judgments do not appear to be manifestations of a coherent, substantive theory of the concept of national identity, they suggest that

40 See also *Kaczorova-Ireland*, What Is the European Union required to Respect under Article 4(2) TEU? The Uniqueness Approach, EPL 25 (2019), 57 (71).

the ECJ has elaborated some kind of an adjudication scheme, and it is adhering to this standard of evaluation. Currently, what the ECJ seems to respect when interpreting Art. 4(2) TEU is the national identity embodied by the domestic legal system from the moment of the foundation of the independent and democratic state. For instance, in the *Sayn-Wittgenstein* case, the ECJ held that the ban on a person using the noble elements of their name constituted a part of the national identity embodied in the legal system of the independent Republic of Austria.[41] Similarly, in the *Bogendorff* case, the ECJ accepted the German constitutional choice to abolish privileges of birth and rank as an element of national identity.[42] And even in the *Runević-Vardyn* case, the ECJ took into account that the Lithuanian language is one of the fundamental constitutional values of independent and democratic Lithuania.[43] All these findings suggest that the ECJ approaches the concept of national identity through the constitutional law framework of the independent and democratic state.

From here, it would take only a small step forward for the ECJ to recognise that only the constitution of a democratic state has a constitutional identity. The constitution that is perceived as a higher regulatory norm and which establishes legitimate authority tied to the protection of human rights, democracy, and the rule of law.[44] Its constitutional identity is shaped

41 ECJ, *Ilonka Sayn-Wittgenstein v. Landeshauptmann von Wien*, C-208/09, ECLI:EU:C:2010:806, paras. 74, 80, 83. *Besselink*, Respecting Constitutional Identity in the EU, Case C-208/09, 22 December 2010, Ilonka Sayn-Wittgenstein v. Landeshauptmann von Wien, CML Rev. 49 (2012), 671.

42 ECJ, *Nabiel Peter Bogendorff von Wolffersdorff v. Standesamt der Stadt Karlsruhe und Zentraler Juristischer Dienst der Stadt Karlsruhe*, C-438/14, ECLI:EU:C:2016:401, para. 64.

43 ECJ, *Malgožata Runević-Vardyn and Łukasz Paweł Wardyn v. Vilniaus miesto savivaldybės administracija and Others*, C-391/09, ECLI:EU:C:2011:291, para. 54. In this case, the ECJ accepted a Member State's argument that the Lithuanian language constitutes a constitutional asset that preserves the nation's identity and held that the specific alphabet constituted a legitimate objective capable of justifying the restrictions on the rights of the Polish minority. It is debatable whether the exclusionist national identity confirmed by the Lithuanian Constitutional Court is compatible with the constitutional core that emanates from EU and domestic constitutional orders. *Kochenov*, When Equality Directives Are Not Enough: Taking an Issue with the Missing Minority Rights Policy in the EU, in: Belavusau/Henrard (eds.), EU Anti-discrimination Law Beyond Gender, 2018, p. 119.

44 One might question the new impact of this suggestion if a democratic state is a prerequisite for entrance into the EU. Yet following the European Parliament's acknowledgement in 2022 that Hungary, one of the Member States, is not a democracy but rather a 'hybrid regime of electoral autocracy', it is crucial to emphasise that it

by the democratic domestic institutions. It is this constitutional identity that EU law should respect. The ECJ may acknowledge that not every national identity claim a Member State presents is a valid claim under EU law, only those claims that are embedded in the domestic constitutional framework and relate to a reasonable interpretation of human rights, democracy, and the rule of law as long as these claims do not contradict EU constitutional commitments.

The question then remains: How can the ECJ perform a review of domestic measures regarding which the protection of national identity is invoked? It is already part of ECJ's case law that even in cases concerning national identity claims, the ECJ conducts a proportionality review to determine if the national measure is justified. The scope of proportionality review, however, has been widely discussed by scholars and practitioners.

Notable scholars contend that the requirement of proportionality limits the concept of national identity, and they argue for a weak procedural rationality test.[45] However, when they maintain that the ECJ should adopt a formal approach, what they have in mind are the cases in which the constitutional courts refer to fundamental rights or inalienable principles that they regard as belonging to the EU Member States' core constitutional identity. The Central European constitutional courts, including the captured Hungarian one, however, often do not invoke the concept of identity in areas that are inside the traditional field of constitutionalism; instead, they invoke it in policy questions, like migration, national security, social security or family law. Those scholars who acknowledge this difference argue for a strict scrutiny test by saying that invocation of national identity in service of limiting fundamental rights is prima facie suspect, given the danger of national identity being deployed to disadvantage or disparately impact already vulnerable minorities.[46]

---

is not evident anymore that EU Member States' constitutional frameworks respect the universal foundational principles of the EU: the protection of human rights, democracy, and the rule of law, European Parliament resolution of 15 September 2022 on the proposal for a Council decision determining, pursuant to Article 7(1) of the Treaty on European Union, the existence of a clear risk of a serious breach by Hungary of the values on which the Union is founded, 2018/0902R(NLE).

45 *Van de Heyning*, The European Perspective: from lingua franca to common language, in: Claes/de Visser/Popelier/Van de Heyning (eds.), Constitutional Conversations in Europe. Actors, Topics and Procedures, 2012, p. 181 (203).

46 *Müller*, Militant Democracy and Constitutional Identity, in: Jacobsohn/Schor (eds.), Comparative Constitutional Theory, 2018, p. 415 (417).

Advocate General *Kokott* takes a third approach: she suggests that the ECJ should distinguish between national measures linked to what she calls the "*fundamental expression of national identity*"[47] and those which concern non-fundamental expressions of national identity. In cases concerning fundamental expressions of national identity, she recommends that the ECJ restrict itself to undertaking limited judicial review based on the requirements arising from Art. 2 TEU. According to her, the ECJ should exclude proportionality because, in this instance, the domestic courts carry out proportionality reviews. For instance, Advocate General *Kokott* argues that the area of family law falls within the scope of fundamental expressions of national identity;[48] thus, the ECJ should restrict the intensity of its review: it should not carry out a proportionality review; it should only review whether the domestic measure is compatible with Art. 2 TEU. Apart from the "*fundamental expression of national identity*"[49], the ECJ should perform full scrutiny on domestic measures justified by the protection of national identity, proportionality included.

Yet, this distinction raises more questions than answers. For instance, in certain cases involving family law (e.g., same-sex marriage, surrogate motherhood, marital name choices), there may be limitations placed on fundamental rights; hence, invoking national identity in these cases is prima facie suspect. Is it appropriate to defer to domestic institutions to conduct a proportionality review? The European Court of Human Rights has already rejected the idea: it condemned Bulgaria for not fulfilling its positive obligation under Art. 8 of the Convention (respect for private life and family life) to establish a legal framework for recognising same-sex marriages performed outside its jurisdiction.[50] Finally, the need for a differentiation between "fundamental" and "non-fundamental expression of

47 *Kokott* (fn. 14), para. 92. Advocate General *Kokott* argues that the ECJ has already implicitly recognised in the *Coman* case that the rules governing marriage form part of national identity. ECJ, *Relu Adrian Coman and Others v. Inspectoratul General pentru Imigrări and Ministerul Afaceriol Interne,* C-673/16, ECLI:EU:C:2018:385, paras. 42-43.

48 The opinion of Advocate General *Kokott* referred to the German Federal Constitutional Court's Lisbon decision, in which the Court held that "*Verfassungsidentität*" does not only encompass the constitutional principles but also family law which is "*considered crucial for the ability of a constitutional democracy to govern itself*", cf. BVerfGE 123, 267 (359) [official translation by the court].

49 *Kokott* (fn. 14), para. 92.

50 ECHR, *Koilova and Babulkova v. Bulgaria* (5.9.2023), App. no. 40209/20.

national identity" is not entirely justified, and it is not apparent why family law constitutes a fundamental aspect of national identity protection.

G. Concluding Remarks

National identity claims are a key factor in shaping our times and the ongoing evolution of the European Union. To assess their impact, this piece focused on the ethnoculturally informed national identity claims and asked how the ECJ can respond to these claims. It argued that the ECJ has the option to interpret "national identity" based on the specific constitutional framework of the Member State in question or regard "national identity" as autonomous. Which direction the ECJ will take is an open question at this point.

Some, like *Dieter Grimm*, argue that ongoing "*constitutionalisation of the treaties*"[51] by the ECJ, as he calls it, actually decreases EU legitimacy. Others assert that the ECJ can exert a rule of law-enhancing role, but that requires a certain thinness of constitutional law.[52] However, to prevent the EU from reverting to an economic alliance of isolated sovereign states with their own agendas, the ECJ, as the final arbiter in EU legal matters, must be empowered to uphold the fundamental values of Art. 2 TEU that form the basis of the EU. Here, I offered one possibility of how the ECJ can best ensure that the universal constitutional principles on which EU law is built continue to be respected when confronted with national identity claims. Hopefully, Europeans will be able to preserve *Hallstein*'s community of law and prevent the takeover of the rule of law by manipulation and violence.

51 *Grimm*, Constitutionalisation without Constitution: A Democracy Problem, in: Barber/Cahill/Ekins (eds.), The Rise and Fall of the European Constitution, 2019, p. 23 (26).

52 *Michelman*, Constitutional Essentials. On the Constitutional Theory of Political Liberalism, 2023, p. 67.

EU Rule of Law from a Human Rights dimension: Case Law in Lithuania

Skirgailė Žaltauskaitė-Žalimienė

A. Introduction

In the light of the practice of international and national courts, as well as the changing situation in Europe, it is easy to assume that the importance of the rule of law and legal certainty is only increasing, and in the current legal environment, more and more attention is being paid to them. It is also expected that the promotion of justice and equality in EU Member States can be facilitated and improved by applying the concepts of the rule of law and respect for human rights.

Among other areas, the rule of law was heavily debated in the context of counter-terrorism measures after September 11, and in the discussion about the compatibility with the rule of law of the actions of Member States supervising illegal immigration at the southern European Union (hereinafter – the EU) borders. The enlargement of the EU to include quite different political cultures and economic backgrounds places emphasis on this principle as a condition of an effective common internal market. However, in recent years, some EU Member States have violated the principle of the rule of law. Over the past five years, we have witnessed a crisis of the rule of law in Poland and Hungary. In addition, European politicians are talking about threats to the judicial system and media pluralism, and consequently to the rule of law in Slovakia, Italy, Bulgaria, and Greece.

There is discussion about the lack of progress on the procedure under Article 7 of the Treaty on European Union (hereinafter – the TEU) procedure, which is the main tool for holding countries accountable if they breach EU values. For most of the past five years, both Hungary and Poland remained stuck in the first stage of the process[1]. In Hungary's case, Member States did not take additional steps towards determining that there is a "*risk*

1 During the publication of the EU's 2024 Rule of Law Report, Commissioner for Values and Transparency *Věra Jourová* highlighted two success stories: the closing of the Article 7 process against Poland and the end of a five-year-long deadlock on judicial appointments in Spain.

of a serious breach" of EU values, the first step of the procedure. When it comes to Poland, the Commission closed the procedure in May 2024. The decision came after Poland's newly elected government proposed plans to remedy violations of the rule of law.

The number of infringement proceedings – the other enforcement tool in the hands of the Commission – has plummeted since the early 2000s, negatively impacting rule of law enforcement. This trend has continued in recent years, although there were some important exceptions[2]. These included record-high fines, handed out to Poland in 2021 for the government's attempt to discipline judges, and to Hungary in 2024 for violating the rights of asylum seekers.

The most important development was the introduction of the so-called conditionality regulation, and the subsequent suspension of EU funding linked to rule of law violations[3]. This rule of law conditionality requires that breaches must affect or seriously risk affecting the sound financial management of the Union budget or the protection of the financial interests of the Union in a sufficiently direct way. In this respect, there is an incongruity between the accent on the principle of the rule of law within the EU legal system and the absence of a consistent mechanism to ensure the unity of Member States in this area.

Modern discussions highlight the crucial role of the rule of law in ensuring adequate respect for human rights[4] and that the rule of law is one of the fundamental values of the EU[5]. However, the importance of implementing

2 *Csaky*, The EU and the rule of law: Much movement, little change, CER Insight, 7.10.2024, available at: https://www.cer.eu/insights/eu-and-rule-law-much-movement-little-change (last access: 23.10.2025).

3 Regulation (EU, Euratom) 2020/2092 of the European Parliament and of the Council of 16 December 2020 on a general regime of conditionality for the protection of the Union budget, OJ LI 433/1; Hungary and Poland voted against it and it is expected that its validity will be challenged before the CJEU via an action for annulment (Article 263 TFEU).

4 In this Article, in accordance with the parlance of the Charter of Fundamental Rights, the terms "*human rights*" and "*fundamental rights*" will be used interchangeably.

5 *Pech/Kochenov*, Respect for the Rule of Law in the Case Law of the European Court of Justice: A Casebook Overview of Key Judgments since the Portuguese Judges Case, 2021; *von Bogdandy/Bogdanowicz/Canor/Taborowski/Schmidt*, A constitutional moment for the European rule of law – upcoming landmark decisions concerning the polish judiciary, MPIL Research Paper No. 2018-10; *Arnold/Martínez-Estay* (eds.), Rule of Law, Human Rights and Judicial Control of Power. Some Reflections from National and International Law, 2017; *Pech/Scheppele*, Illiberalism Within: Rule of Law Backsliding in the EU, 2017, Cambridge Yearbook of European Legal Studies 19

the rule of law in relation to human rights remains pertinent. It is important to note that the necessity to adhere to the principle of the rule of law is articulated in the preambles of both the European Convention on Human Rights and the EU Charter of Fundamental Rights. Therefore, it is vital for states to incorporate the rule of law within their national legal systems to protect human rights effectively. Indeed, human rights violations can arise from the inadequacy of the rule of law in democratic states. Within this context, the ongoing discourse on how the rule of law can strengthen the protection of human rights should be regarded as particularly timely.

The purpose of the following article is to explore the intricate relationship between the rule of law and respect for human rights in the evolving legal order and the main focus will be on the relevant case law of Lithuanian courts. This article will discuss two seemingly abstract issues, namely the general principle of the rule of law in case law and the definition of the rule of law in recent legislation. The core analysis of this paper will focus on assessing the compatibility of case law with the rule of law and human rights principles, along with identifying possible challenges in the current legal system.

Since the beginning of the European integration process, the EU has upheld high and effective standards for the protection of fundamental rights. What initially emerged as an obligation to align with the Convention on Human Rights has evolved into a comprehensive framework for rights protection and a well-defined policy grounded in respect for fundamental rights. The development of the rule of law as a constitutional requirement and a cornerstone of the legal order has been equally complex, if not more so. This article also examines whether the rule of law, as conceptualised by the EU, serves as a prerequisite for safeguarding fundamental rights and explores possible ways to enhance its effectiveness.

(2017), 3-47; *Pech*, The Rule of Law in the EU: The Evolution of the Treaty Framework and Rule of Law Toolbox, RECONNECT Working Paper No. 7 (March 2020); *Milašiūtė/Žalimienė*, European standards of judicial independence in Lithuania, East European yearbook on human rights 2021, 25-51.

B. Conceptual Framework

I. The Rule of Law and Human Rights

The principles of the rule of law become a significant legal foundation of the European Community *acquis communautaire*[6]. The rule of law, aside from its judicial dimension, implies also political, institutional, social, economic and even a policy of memory aspects. The rule of law brings together a range of areas that are interlinked, complementary and cannot be understood as separate subsets. In other words, a deficiency in one subsystem of the rule of law leads to deficiencies in other subsystems. The rule of law empowers respect for the principles and standards that the legal areas must follow in order to ensure rights and freedoms. Given that the rule of law naturally incorporates respect for human rights, it remains a key pillar of its foundation.

The Court of Justice constitutionalized fundamental rights in a Community and recognized that fundamental rights have the same legal value as the general principles of Community law. In accordance with Article 6(1) of the TEU, the Union recognises the rights, freedoms and principles set out in the Charter of Fundamental Rights of the European Union (hereinafter – the Charter), as adapted by the Treaty of Lisbon, which has the same legal value as the founding Treaties. This means that the provisions of the Charter are classified in the category of primary law, even if those provisions are not integrated into the Treaties and form a self-standing document. At the same time, the provisions of the Charter fall within the ambit of the constitutional principles of the founding Treaties, which constitute the supreme part of the EU law. As to fundamental rights enshrined in the Charter, the same rules, which have been formulated regarding fundamental rights guaranteed as general principles of law, apply[7].

In the context of the EU's accession to the ECHR, it should be noted that the CJEU had decided on the issue of and found legal problems with a potential EU accession to the ECHR twice in EU history[8].

---

6 *von Danwitz*, Values and the Rule of Law: Foundations of the European Union – An Inside Perspective from the ECJ, April 2018, PER / PELJ 2018 (21).

7 *Jarass*, Charta der Grundrechte der Europäischen Union. Kommentar, 2. ed., 2013, p. 7.

8 ECJ, *Opinion 1/91 (Accession I)*, ECR 1991, I-6079; ECJ, *Opinion 2/13 (Accession II)*, ECLI:EU:C:2014:2454; *Kochenov*, EU Law without the Rule of Law: Is the Veneration of Autonomy Worth It?, Yearbook of European Law 34 (2015), 74; *Grogan/Pech*, The crystallisation of a core EU meaning of the rule of law and its (limited) normative

Human rights prove to be the basis of EU law and have been recognised as the common values shared by the Member States in accordance with Article 6(3) TEU. The Member States have a duty to ensure their protection and respect. The rule of law can only be fully observed in a system that respects human rights and fundamental freedoms and ensures the protection of individual rights. The recognition of human rights reinforces the transparency and accountability of the authorities and guarantees a fair trial procedure. It is generally accepted that human rights have a universal dimension that overrides the rights or interests of the State.

II. The Rule of Law as a Practical Concept: international courts' approach

The Statute of the Council of Europe refers to the rule of law twice: in the Preamble, where the signatory Governments affirm their devotion to the rule of law, and in Article 3, which provides that every member must accept the principles of the rule of law. In the Convention on Human Rights, the reference is made once: in the Preamble.

The principle of the rule of law seems simple at first glance, but, when one attempts to explore its conceptual scope and content, things become quite complex. However, in the landmark judgment in *Golder v. the United Kingdom* of 1975[9], the ECHR made clear that the rule of law under the Convention is "*one of the features of the common spiritual heritage*" of the Member States of the Council of Europe. It is from the rule of law which the whole Convention draws inspiration. It is a principle "*underlying the Convention*" along with the "*avoidance of arbitrary power*"[10].

The ECHR has consistently held that the principle of the rule of law is inherent in all the Articles of the Convention[11], the Court's finding that the rule of law is "*inherent*" in all the Articles of the Convention means that the principle provides for a methodological point of departure in the examination of any arguable Convention complaint whilst at the same time creating a frame of reference when the Court interprets and applies the

influence beyond the EU, RECONNECT: Work Package 7, 2021, available at: https://papers.ssrn.com/sol3/papers.cfm?abstract_id=4093034 (last access: 23.10.2025).

9 ECHR, *Golder v. the United Kingdom* (21.2.1975), App. no. 4451/70, para. 34, 21.

10 *Spano*, The rule of law as the lodestar of the European Convention on Human Rights: The Strasbourg Court and the independence of the judiciary, European Law Journal 27 (2021), 211-227.

11 ECHR, *Pişkin v. Turkey* (15.12.2020), App. no. 33399/18, para. 153.

rights and freedoms provided for by the Convention[12]. The rule of law thus is conceived as the opposite of arbitrariness and part of the spirit of the Convention[13].

As noted by *Dean Spielmann*, former President of the European Court of Human Rights (hereinafter – the ECHR), "*by defending the rule of law and ruling on cases that go to the heart of the Member States' constitutional arrangements, the Court of Justice of the European Union* (hereinafter – the CJEU) *is defending the vision of a liberal democracy against the backdrop of an economic, political and migratory crisis, which is still ongoing in a number of European Union Member States*"[14].

However, most of the early rule of law definitions produced by the Court of Justice provide a thin and teleological interpretation of the rule of law, which prioritises the attainment of *European Economic Community* (hereinafter – EEC) goals with little regard to the position of the individual and their rights[15]. The *Les Verts* case[16] instead, constitutes the first explicit judgment that defines the rule of law as a fundamental principle of EU law. Accordingly, the rule of law entails that neither its Member States nor its institutions can avoid a review of the question whether the measures adopted by them are in conformity with the basic constitutional charter, the treaty. This reveals a thin definition of the rule of law in which, the key to the notion of the rule of law is the reviewability of decisions of public authorities by independent courts[17].

The rule of law is one of the overarching values of the European Union listed in Article 2 TEU. It is legally material in a number of respects. As one of the values, it has a strong sense of signaling and interpretation, *part of the identity of the Union*. Adherence to the rule of law is a *sine qua non*

12 *Spano* (fn. 10); ECHR Judge and President of Section, Siofra O'Leary, has argued that "[ever] since *Golder v. the United Kingdom*, the court has used the rule of law as an interpretative tool for the development of substantive guarantees set forth in the Convention"; see 'Europe and the Rule of Law', in: Bobek/Prass (eds.), The EU Charter of Fundamental Rights in the Member States, 2020, p. 37 (60).

13 *Kūris*, On the rule of law and the quality of the law: reflections of the constitutional-turned-international judge, Teoría y Realidad Constitucional 42 (2018), 131-159.

14 *Spielmann*, The Rule of Law Principle in the Jurisprudence of the Court of Justice of the European Union, in: Elósegui/Miron/Motoc (eds.), The Rule of Law in Europe: Recent Challenges and Judicial Responses, 2021, p. 3-20.

15 *Saenz Perez*, What about fundamental rights? Security and fundamental rights in the midst of a rule of law breakdown, New Journal of European Criminal Law 13 (2022), 526-545.

16 ECJ, *Parti écologiste 'Les Verts'/European Parliament*, C-294/83, ECLI:EU:C:1986:166.

17 *Jacobs*, The sovereignty of law: The European way, 2007, p. 35.

condition for a state to join the Union and failure by a Member State to comply with it may give rise to a special enforcement procedure. Also, in combination with Article 19(1) TEU, it has been used to impose obligations on Member States regarding their system of governance, especially judicial independence. Here, commitment to Article 2 TEU creates governance expectations that permeate the national legal system and apply beyond the material scope of the EU Charter.

The values of democratic constitutionalism, including the rule of law, are most clearly reflected in the substantial body of case law from the CJEU regarding judicial independence and the European Commission's intensified efforts to address rule of law violations. This topic is extremely important because by establishing the rule of law and having an independent judiciary to uphold the rule of law will result in the creation of greater respect for human rights[18].

In the context of the rule of law, the importance of judicial independence has been elevated and become more enforceable within the EU legal nexus in recent years in response to the rule of law crisis that has been growing in the Union for the last decade. The Court of Justice has played a titular role in bolstering the rule of law value through its case law recently. This is particularly evident in the cases of *Trade Union of Portuguese Judges*[19], *L. M.*[20] and *A. K. and Others v. Sąd Najwyższy*[21], which arose from the preliminary ruling procedure of Article 267 of the Treaty on the Functioning of the European Union (hereinafter – the TFEU).

These three cases have had a profound impact on the rule of law battle as together they have made the rule of law under Article 2 TEU a legally enforceable value with a minimum set of requirements that Member States cannot ignore. The judgments in these cases, together with the new Rule of Law Mechanism and Rule of Law Reports, elaborated on the principles of judicial independence and the rule of law as well as their importance within individual Member States and how they uphold the EU judicial system.

In *Trade Union of Portuguese Judges* the Court of Justice decided that the budgetary measures which reduced the salaries of the judges of the

---

18 *Shumate*, Key Ingredients in the Rule of Law Recipe: The Role of Judicial Independence in the Effective Establishment of the Rule of Law, available at: https://scholarcommons.usf.edu/etd/5126 (last access: 23.10.2025).

19 ECJ, *Associação Sindical dos Juízes Portugueses*, C-64/16, ECLI:EU:C:2017:395.

20 ECJ, *LM*, C-216/18 PPU, ECLI:EU:C:2018:586.

21 ECJ (GC), *A.K. (Indépendance de la chambre disciplinaire de la Cour suprême)*, joined cases C-585/18, C-624/18 and C-625/18, ECLI:EU:C:2019:982.

Tribunal de Contas did not violate their judicial independence as these reductions were temporary and affected public sector workers in general and were not specific to judges. However, a key aspect of this judgement is the Court's robust language in articulating the value of judicial independence within the EU. The Court explains that the rule of law, as expressed in Article 2 TEU, is assumed to be a common value held by all Member States. Article 19 TEU "gives concrete expression" to the value of the rule of law and "entrusts the responsibility for ensuring judicial review in the EU legal order not only to the Court of Justice but also to national courts and tribunals".

The *L.M.* case originated in Ireland, where the High Court was called to give execution to a European Arrest Warrant (hereinafter – EAW) issued by Poland against Mr. A. C., accused of drug-related offences. The Irish Court doubted whether, in view of the systemic deficiencies with the rule of law in Poland, the execution of the EAW could lead to the violation of the applicant's fundamental right to a fair trial, protected by the Irish Constitution, the ECHR and the EU Charter of Fundamental Rights. In this case, the Court balanced, on the one hand, the general values, such as the rule of law and fundamental rights, which are important for the entire Union and, on the other hand, the need to ensure the smooth functioning of mutual trust measures. The CJEU conceded that a Commission proposal addressed to the Council to determine a "*clear risk of serious breach*" of EU values by the accused country as set out in Art. 7(1) TEU could indicate the fulfilment of the systemic and generalised deficiencies, that would imply a lack of mutual trust.

In the *A.K.* case, the CJEU found that the Polish judicial reform threatened the independence of the courts, for example through the politically controlled disciplinary chamber. The CJEU laid down criteria for determining whether the new disciplinary boards should be regarded as judicial authorities within the meaning of Article 47 of the EU Charter of Fundamental Rights and Article 6 of the ECHR.

In 2022 the European Commission launched infringement proceedings against Hungary[22], alleging, among other things, a direct violation of Article 2 TEU. This sparked debate among lawyers as to whether the CJEU might develop its case law to allow Article 2 TEU to serve as an independent legal basis, even without a connection to specific EU law provisions. This infringement action targets the so-called "anti-LGBTQ+ law" passed

22 ECJ, pending case C-769/22.

in 2021. It is the first time that the Commission expressly mentions Article 2 TEU as a self-standing ground. This decision represents a further step in how the Union is dealing with the "rule of law crisis" as a consequence of the tendencies manifested by Member States such as Poland and Hungary challenging the concept of rule of law and in particular, Article 2 TEU.

The Court of Justice has with sincerity brought to life the values on which the Union rests, applying them on a case-by-case basis to the disputes brought to its attention[23]. It is clear that we can talk about the real added value that the Court brings to the citizens of the Union by developing the principle of the rule of law in its case law.

More than fifty years ago, the CJEU famously held in the *Van Gend en Loos* case[24] that the judicial protection of EU rights is based on a system of dual vigilance. In addition to the supervision carried out by the European Commission and the Member States, individuals are entitled to rely on their EU rights in the national courts. In cooperation with the Court of Justice, they have relied on EU law in order to provide effective remedies to the rights that the law confers on individuals[25]. We cannot therefore ignore the important role that national courts play in ensuring the rule of law in the EU.

III. The Rule of Law as a Fundamental and Binding Value within Europe

In the context of defining the rule of law, it should be noted that at the European level, the Council of Europe's Commission for Democracy through Law, known as the Venice Commission, draws on Lord Bingham's definition. In its 2011 "Report on the Rule of Law", the Venice Commission considered the historical origins of the Rule of law and related concepts of '*Etat de droit*' and '*Rechtsstaat*', as well as instances of the concept of the Rule of Law at national and international levels. It was also careful to distinguish the 'Rule of Law' from 'Rule by Law', which it described as "a purely formalistic concept under which any action of a public official which is authorised by law is said to fulfil its requirements". According to

23 *von Danwitz* (fn. 6).

24 ECJ, *Van Gend & Loos*, C-26/62, ECLI:EU:C:1963:1.

25 *Lenaerts*, New Horizons for the Rule of Law Within the EU, German Law Journal 21 (2020), 29-34.

the Venice Commission, the Rule of Law is primarily concerned with the protection and promotion of human rights[26].

It is also notable that Conditionality Regulation No. 2020/2092[27] provides a comprehensive definition of the rule of law, under which it includes: "*the principles of legality, implying a transparent, accountable, democratic and pluralistic law-making process; legal certainty; prohibition of arbitrariness of the executive powers; effective judicial protection, including access to justice, by independent and impartial courts, also as regards fundamental rights; separation of powers; and non-discrimination and equality before the law.*"

According to the European Law Institute (hereinafter – ELI)[28] Charter of Fundamental Constitutional Principles of European Democracy[29], the principles of the independence of the judiciary, the checks and balances of accountability, dignity and equality, and the protection of fundamental rights, are all integral parts of the rule of law.

Providing a clear definition of the rule of law is not an easy task. This concept, which is central to the EU, can still be defined in very different ways by academics, lawyers, judges and other actors such as the European Council, the European Parliament and the European Commission. Thus, treating the rule of law as 'the very essence of law', different interpretations of this principle are to be expected[30]. The rule of law requires law to be predictable, accessible and uniformly applied. As a prelude to any consideration of functionality, efficiency or effectiveness, it is necessary to touch on these minimum requirements *prima facie*.

As previously mentioned, the rule of law constitutes one of the Union's core values, which must be upheld within the national legal systems of all Member States. It is important to recognize and it is widely acknowledged,

---

26 Venice Commission's Report on the Rule of Law, 25/26 March 2011, CDL-AD (2011) 003rev.

27 Regulation 2020/2092 of 16 December 2020 (fn. 3), so-called "Rule of Law Conditionality Regulation".

28 The European Law Institute (ELI) is an independent non-profit organisation established to initiate, conduct and facilitate research, make recommendations and provide practical guidance in the field of European legal development.

29 Charter of principles seek to encapsulate contemporary European constitutionalism, available at: https://europeanlawinstitute.eu/fileadmin/user_upload/p_eli/Publications/ELI_Charter_of_Fundamental_Constitutional_Principles_of_a_European_Democracy.pdf (last access: 23.10.2025).

30 *Webber*, Legal reasoning and Bills of Rights, LSE Law, Society and Economy Working Papers 1/2011.

that the rule of law is a firmly established principle. Despite the varying national identities, legal systems, and traditions across Member States, the fundamental essence of the rule of law should remain consistent throughout the EU.

The rule of law is a foundational value within the EU and is enshrined in founding treaty provisions. These provisions, such as Articles 2 and 19 of the TEU, in combination with Articles 258, 259, and 260 of the TFEU, oblige Member States to ensure EU law is respected by implementing effective remedy procedures resulting in sanctions where infringement is established by the Court of Justice[31]. This ensures the harmonious functioning of the EU legal order and underlines its autonomous legal system. The rule of law, the respect of human rights and the general principles of EU law are binding on Member States, as enshrined in Article 51(1) of the Charter, which implies a systemic nature embracing the whole EU legal architecture. The rule of law is part of the *common values* of the EU that are enshrined in Article 2 TEU, legally enforceable under Article 7(1) TEU through a procedure that may ultimately lead to a *sanctions regime.*

The Conditionality Regulation establishes a conditionality mechanism protecting the Union budget. The Regulation consists of ten articles, accompanied by 29 recitals. Art. 2(1)(a) of the Regulation defines the terms "*rule of law*" as referring to the "*Union value in art. 2 TEU* (...) [which] *shall be understood having regard to the other Union values and principles enshrined in art. 2 TEU*". The values of the Union have been derived by the Court of Justice from the constitutional traditions of the Member States.

Violations of the common values of Art. 2 TEU are subject to the Art. 7 TEU procedure[32], other infringements of the Treaties (except those of the obligation of unsound budgetary policies (Art. 126(10) TFEU)) are subject to infringement actions (Art. 258 TFEU)[33]. Thus, a major point of criticism of the Regulation has been the alleged overlap with both these procedures.

---

31 *Berkes*, The extraterritorial human rights obligations of the EU in its external trade and investment policies, [2018] 2(1): 5. Europe and the World: A Law Review [21].

32 *Closa*, Institutional Logics and the EU's Limited Sanctioning Capacity under Article 7 TEU, International Political Science Review 42 (2020), 501.

33 *Scheppele*, Enforcing the Basic Principles of EU Law through Systemic Infringement Actions, in: Closa/Kochenov (eds.), Reinforcing Rule of Law Oversight in the European Union, 2016, p. 105; *Staudinger*, The Rise and Fall of Rule of Law Conditionality, in: Bonelli/Claes/Witte/Podstawa (eds.), Usual and Unusual Suspects: New Actors, Roles and Mechanisms to Protect EU Values, European Papers 7 (2022) [No. 2], p. 721-737.

The case law of the CJEU and the ECHR similarly reveals an understanding of the rule of law as a structuring principle which these courts must always take into account in their day-to-day adjudicative role with a view of strengthening concrete compliance with it, and as an 'umbrella principle'[34] from which judges may derive formal and substantive components or subprinciples. The rule of law, as interpreted by the CJEU, is a broad concept influencing both EU and national legal orders. It encompasses the entire set of norms, principles and grounds that compose the normative framework in which the Member States must act when implementing EU law.

The CJEU and the ECHR have recognised that the rule of law encompasses principles such as: the principle of legality, which refers to a transparent, accountable, democratic and pluralistic legislative process; the principle of legal certainty; the prohibition of the arbitrary exercise of executive powers; effective judicial protection by independent and impartial courts, effective judicial review and respect for fundamental rights; the principle of the separation of powers; the principle of equality before the law (Rule of Law Report[35], 2020, p. 2). It is emphasized that, according to the principle of the rule of law, all powers are always exercised within the limits set by law, respecting the values of democracy and fundamental rights, and under the supervision of independent and impartial judiciary (Rule of Law Report, 2020, p. 2). The rule of law, as interpreted by the CJEU, undoubtedly ensures that the relationship between EU law and the national legal order is shielded from arbitrariness and unfettered power.

Well-functioning, efficient and fully independent justice systems are crucial for the application and enforcement of EU and national law and upholding the rule of law. Judicial independence is integral to the task of judicial decision-making and stems from the principle of effective judicial

---

34 *Marshall*, The Rule of Law. Its Meaning, Scope and Problems, Cahiers de philosophie politique et juridique 24 (1993), 43.

35 On reports on the rule of law: the Commission commits to deepening the EU's monitoring of Rule of Law developments in the Member States through a Rule of Law Review Cycle, the results of which would be published in an annual Rule of Law Report summarising the situation in the Member States; it would also further develop the EU Justice Scoreboard to improve its coverage of Rule of Law related areas; *European Commission*, Communication from the Commission to the European Parliament, the European Council, the Council, the European Economic and Social Committee and the Committee of the Regions: Strengthening the Rule of Law within the Union. A Blue print for Action, 17.7.2019, COM(2019) 343 final.

protection[36] (Rule of Law Report, 2024, p. 10). Ultimately, judicial review constitutes an instrument to guarantee the uniform interpretation and supremacy of EU law, which were essential to achieve the completion of the internal market[37].

IV. The Relationship between the Rule of Law and Human Rights

The EU is based on legal values such as democracy, equality, and human dignity. These values are the foundation of the EU and are set out in the TEU. All EU Members States share an aspiration to safeguard and promote democracy, the rule of law, and human rights. The effective operation of the rule of law is a fundamental component of a functioning, independent state. This is why, over the last two decades, EU Member States have become even more committed to the fundamental principles that bind them together. Human rights protection is also a fundamental element of the rule of law and EU law under the TEU. In this respect, the CJEU emphasizes the interconnectedness of these legal values, demonstrating how each is essential in relation to the others.

However, discussions on the relationship between the rule of law and human rights vary. Some critics argue that the rule of law can only be one of many values that can be implemented selectively, and therefore question its effectiveness in ensuring human rights and point to possible contradictions between these two fundamental principles. Some authors consider that undoubted moral importance of human rights does not sanctify human rights law, which, like any other set of legal rules, is open to question and criticism and should comply with the demands of the rule of law; and human rights law is hard to reconcile with the rule of law, save by a kind of definitional fiat in which human rights law is asserted to be necessary to protect human rights which are asserted in turn to be a constituent part of the rule of law[38].

---

36 Also of relevance, Article 19 of the TEU, and Article 47 of the Charter of Fundamental Rights.

37 *Saenz Perez* (fn. 15).

38 *Ekins*, Human Rights and the Rule of Law, Policy Exchange, 2024, available at: https://policyexchange.org.uk/wp-content/uploads/Human-Rights-and-the-Rule-of-Law.pdf (last access: 23.10.2025).

The principle of the rule of law has deep philosophical and political dimensions[39]. It may therefore be difficult to answer the question of whether the principle of the rule of law strengthens the EU legal order, including its general principles, together with fundamental rights. However, the legal and policy documents produced by the EU and the Council of Europe promote a broad, substantive and holistic understanding of the rule of law[40]. It would be difficult to deny the inherent link between the rule of law and human rights. In other words, the rule of law is generally understood as a principle that includes substantive components (e.g. equality before the law) as well as formal procedural elements (e.g. legal certainty, judicial review), and which requires a democratic and liberal constitutional order giving full effect to human rights[41]. Provisions of the rule of law are considered to be 'a constitutional principle inherent in all clauses' and 'procedural values' – all the principles designed to ensure the democratic functioning of the state. The highly important role of justice in the respect of the rule of law is that everyone is entitled to a fair and public hearing within a reasonable time by an independent and impartial tribunal established by law. Various related issues, such as the assessment of specific situations, harmonization, clarity, accessibility, trust, the protection of legitimate expectations, res judicata, the proportionality test and the protection of citizens against abuse, are relevant to the application of the rule of law. Rights of standing and access to justice vary widely between Member States, and not every individual with a valid claim can muster the necessary resources to activate the legal system and sustain a challenge. This suggests that there is a potential gap between the availability of rights and their actual application[42]. This concerns the functioning of justice, but the rule of law, undoubtedly, is the key part in it. The rule of law requires independent courts that provide fair and fearless adjudication. A further interaction can be sought in the opposite direction: How do human rights contribute to reinforcing and emphasizing the rule of law?

---

39 *Pech*, The Rule of Law as a Well-Established and Well-Defined Principle of EU Law, Hague Journal on the Rule of Law 14 (2022), 107-138, available at: https://link.springer.com/article/10.1007/s40803-022-00176-8 (last access: 23.10.2025).

40 *Grogan/Pech* (fn. 8).

41 *Pech* (fn. 39).

42 *Hofmann*, No longer gatekeeper: Why the European Commission provides access to justice for civil society organisations, Paper to be presented at the EUSA Fourteenth Biennial Conference in Boston, March 5-7 2015.

C. EU Rule of Law from a Human Rights Dimension: Case Law in Lithuania

I. International Human Rights Standards in Lithuania

The Constitutional Act on Membership of the Republic of Lithuania in the European Union (Article 2) indicates that the norms of EU law are a constituent part of the legal system of the Republic of Lithuania; insofar as founding EU treaties are concerned EU law applies directly, and, in the event of a conflict of laws, have supremacy over the laws and other legal acts of the Republic of Lithuania.

The ruling of the Constitutional Court of the Republic of Lithuania (hereinafter – the Constitutional Court) of 14 March 2006 elaborates on the primacy of EU law in relation to the provisions of Lithuanian legislation: first, the Constitutional Court refers to the constitutional principle requiring to apply an international agreement when national law sets out a legal regulation which competes with one laid down in this treaty; second, the same principle applies to EU law, as the Constitution[43] expressly establishes a conflict-of-law rule that gives priority to the application of EU law in cases where EU law arising from the founding treaties of the EU competes with the legal rules laid down in Lithuanian national legislation (regardless of their legal force), with the exception of the Constitution itself.

E. Kūris states that the aforementioned ruling of the Constitutional Court presents the 'designed' algorithm of coexistence between EU law and constitutional law of Lithuania which, on the one hand, recognises political realities relating to the aim of deeper European integration and does not preclude the corresponding legal process, and, on the other hand, does not sacrifice the primacy of the Constitution and the hierarchy of laws arising thereof[44]. *E. Jarašiūnas* believes that the primacy of the Constitution was and remains intact, i.e. Lithuania participates in the process of European integration only relying on its own Constitution that has been and remains the highest national law. According to *Jarašiūnas*, due to the fact that the Constitution and EU law are grounded on common values, all the preconditions exist for the coordination of national and European law. Only a sustainable application of national law, grounded on the Constitution and

---

43 Constitution of the Republic of Lithuania, 25 October 1992.

44 *Kūris*, Europos Sąjungos teisė Lietuvos Respublikos Konstitucinio teismo jurisprudencijoje: sambūvio algoritmo paieškos, in: Katuoka (ed.), Teisė besikeičiančioje Europoje. Liber Amicorum Pranas Kūris, 2008, p. 682-683.

EU law, can ensure a successful alignment process of European countries[45]. On the relationship between EU law and the Constitution, *Kūris* stresses the importance of "*a friendly two-way interpretation*", where the two legal systems can overlap in their jurisprudence[46].

Consequently, the case law of the Constitutional Court, based on the provisions of the Constitution, and the position of academics on the relationship between EU law and the Constitution are essentially consistent with the concept of the primacy of EU law as developed in the case law of the CJEU. On the other hand, it should be noted that the CJEU in its case law as well as the other EU institutions do not aim to exacerbate the tension in relationship between the EU law and national constitutions[47]. Both the CJEU and the national courts are considered to be satisfied with the above-mentioned path of a friendly two-way interpretation. In opting for this friendly two-way interpretation, courts must strike a balance between the principles of laws which are common for the European tradition of law.

The Constitutional Court has stated that the full participation of Lithuania as a member of the EU is a constitutional imperative based on the expression of the sovereign will of the Nation, and that the full membership of Lithuania in the EU is a constitutional value[48]. The constitutional principle of full participation in the European Union necessitates Lithuania's commitment to properly implementing the requirements of EU law[49]. EU law serves as a source for interpreting the law of the Republic of Lithuania, including the Constitution, in areas where, pursuant to Article 1 of the Constitutional Act 'On the Membership of the Republic of Lithuania in

---

45 *Jarašiūnas*, Kelios mintys apie Lietuvos dalyvavimo tarptautiniuose santykiuose konstituciniai pagrindai, in: Liber Amicorum Pranas Kūris (fn. 44), p. 613-644.

46 *Kūris* (fn. 44), p. 694; Jarukaitis (2012), Europos žmogaus teisių konvencija ir Europos Sąjungos teisė: požiūrių konvergencija Baltijos valstybių teismų praktikoje, in: Žmogus, teisinė valstybė ir administracinė justicija. Lietuvos vyriausiasis administracinis teismas, 2012, p. 156-195; Jarukaitis/Švedas, The Constitutional Experience of Lithuania in the Context of European and Global Governance Challenges, in: Albi/Bardutzky (eds.), National Constitutions in European and Global Governance: Democracy, Rights, the Rule of Law, 2019.

47 Also *Žaltauskaitė-Žalimienė*, Fundamental Rights of the European Union: The Jurisprudence of the Supreme Administrative Court of Lithuania, in: *Žaltauskaitė-Žalimienė/Treigė* (eds.), European Union Law and Lithuanian Administrative Justice: A collection of scholarly articles to commemorate a 20 year anniversary of the Supreme Administrative Court of Lithuania, 2023, p. 106-139.

48 Constitutional Court Ruling of 24 January 2014, Ruling of 16 May 2016, Ruling of 14 December 2018, etc.

49 Constitutional Court Ruling of 14 December 2018, Ruling of 11 January 2019, etc.

the European Union', the Republic of Lithuania shares or delegates the competence of state institutions to the EU[50].

International legal acts have become an important source of law, the standard which is used in adjudicating cases at the Supreme Administrative Court of Lithuania (hereinafter – SACL)[51]. Also, the direct applicability of the Convention on Human Rights in case decisions is recognized, with its priority established in the event of a conflict with national laws[52].

For example, in its judgement of 7 May 2010, an administrative case, locally also known as the "Gay pride"[53], the SACL directly applied Article

---

50 Constitutional Court Decision of 20 December 2017, Rulings of 11 January 2019 and 6 February 2020.

51 Regarding the International Covenant on Civil and Political Rights (CCPR), a Decision of 12 May 2021, No. A-671-756/2021 G. J. should be taken into account. The decision was taken, when the proceedings were reopened after the decision of The United Nations Human Rights Committee in 2019, establishing a violation of the right to enter public service on an equal basis, enshrined in Article 25 of the CCPR. The Supreme Administrative Court had to decide, whether violations of the CCPR affected the validity and legality of administrative court decisions previously adopted in the case. In the Decision of 6 March 2014, No. R-525-8-14, the court relied on the CCPR and found that although this covenant establishes guarantees related to the elections to the executive power, it does not prohibit the countries from establishing reasonable restrictions. The court stated that in this case the applicant was subject to a restriction to participate in the Presidential elections, considering that the period, which has passed since the beginning of this restriction, is not obviously disproportionate. In these circumstances, a conclusion of 25 March 2014 of the Human Rights Committee was important. The conclusion provided that the State, Party to the Covenant, had violated the rights of the applicant enshrined in points b) and c) of Article 25 of the CCPR. The applicant requested to reopen the proceedings, claiming that the above-mentioned conclusion of the Human Rights Committee proved that the court did not properly apply provisions of substantive law in his case. However, the case was not reopened (Decision of the Supreme Administrative Court No. P-492-71-14).
Certain decisions, regarding the Convention on Access to Information, Public Participation in Decision-making, and the Right to Apply to Courts in Environmental Matters (Aarhus Convention), are also worth mentioning – 26 May 2021 Decision No. eA-1115-789/2021, 23 September 2013 Decision No. A[520]-211/2013, 19 December 2013 Decision No. A[822]-989/2013.

52 See, e.g., Decision of 11 February 2003 No. 259-03, Decision of 14 April 2008 No. A[575]-164/08, where the Court concluded that through direct application of the Convention and jurisprudence of the ECHR, Lithuania implements the decision of the ECHR and does not perform unlawful activities that manifest in non-implementation of the decision.

53 In a 7 May 2010 Decision No. AS[822]-339/2010, the Court had decided that although the case was on the lawfulness of provisionary measures, it was necessary to examine the case on its merits. If the dispute regarding the lawfulness to organize a march "For

11 of the Convention on Human Rights and relied on the practice of the ECHR in the case *Bączkowski and others v. Poland*[54]. The Court annulled the interim measures of suspension of the validity of the order authorising the demonstration imposed by the Court of First Instance, finding that the interim measures were neither appropriate nor proportionate to the objective pursued, having regard to the positive obligations of the State to ensure that minorities effectively exercise their freedom of assembly.

In the administrative case *R.S. v. the Republic of Lithuania*[55], the Supreme Administrative Court of Lithuania found a violation of Article 8 of the Convention on Human Rights (right to respect for private and family life) due to the failure to establish the appropriate legal mechanisms (adoption of appropriate national legislation) for access to health care in the event of gender reassignment, as well as the lack of effective legal recognition of the applicant's changed identity, and awarded non-pecuniary damages.

It should be emphasised that if national legislation is contrary to the provisions of the ECHR, Lithuanian courts have the authority to base their judgments on the Convention, as it provides an overarching framework for human rights protection. In such cases, the court can interpret domestic laws in a way that ensures they comply with the ECHR. A notable example of this can be found in a case where the media reported on the public procurement process and disclosed the ties between the sole shareholder of the winning company and an employee of the municipality's company responsible for organizing the procurement. The Supreme Administrative Court considered whether the publication of this information violated data protection regulations under the General Data Protection Regulation (GDPR). In doing so, the Court referred to the principles of the European Convention on Human Rights, specifically Article 10, which guarantees the right to freedom of expression[56]. The Court applied the standards set out by the Convention to determine whether the publication of personal data was justified by the public interest.

When ensuring justice and protection of human rights, the Supreme Administrative Court of Lithuania also applies legal provisions and the

---

Equality" had not been examined on its merits by the scheduled day of the march, the suspension of the validity of the permission to organize the march would have denied an essential condition for the effective use of the right of assembly, based on the practice of the ECHR.

54 ECHR, *Bączkowski et al. v. Poland* (3.5.2007), App. No. 1543/06.

55 SACL, Judgment of 29 November 2010, No. A^{858}-1452/2010.

56 SACL, Judgment of 3 February 2022, No. eA-51-822/2022.

catalog of fundamental rights of the EU[57]. As it was already mentioned before, according to the Constitutional Act 'On the Membership of the Republic of Lithuania in the European Union', the legal provisions of the EU are an integral part of the legal system of the Republic of Lithuania. EU law also applies directly, and, in the event of a conflict of laws, has supremacy over the regulations of the Republic of Lithuania.

The issue of the direct application of EU law, including the EU Charter of Fundamental Rights, arose in a case concerning recognition of professional qualifications. The Supreme Administrative Court dealt with a situation, where an applicant had in fact fulfilled all requirements for obtaining professional qualification of a pharmacist, under Section 7 Article 44 of Directive 2005/36/EC, but the professional qualification was not granted to her for purely formal reasons – she did not possess a proof of her professional qualification. The applicant could not obtain such a proof, because due to complex personal circumstances she had fulfilled the requirements to obtain the qualification not in a single Member State, which is ordinarily the case, but in several EU Member States taking advantage of a fundamental EU freedom – free movement of persons. SACL applied to the CJEU for a preliminary ruling on the interpretation of Articles 45, 49 TFEU and Article 15 of the EU Charter of Fundamental Rights and Directive 2005/36/EC[58]. In the ruling C-166/20, *BB v. Ministry of Health of the Republic of Lithuania* of 8 July 2021[59] the CJEU decided that in accordance to the facts of the case, the interpretation of Article 15 Paragraph 2 of the Charter coincides with the interpretation of Articles 45 and 49 of the TFEU and they have to be interpreted in a manner that where a person has acquired professional competence related to this profession both in the Member State of origin and in the host Member State and does not possess a proof of formal qualification, the competent authorities of the host Member State must assess this competence and compare it with the requirements of the host Member State that are necessary to be a pharmacist. In the light of the preliminary ruling the Supreme Administrative Court applied Articles 45 and 49 of the TFEU directly and granted the appellate complaint[60].

---

57 *Žaltauskaitė-Žalimienė*, Europos Sąjungos pagrindinių teisių chartijos taikymas supra- ir nacionaliniu lygmenimis, in: Collective monograph, 2019, p. 39-44.

58 SACL, Ruling of 8 April 2020 in administrative case No. eA-3312-822/2020.

59 ECJ, *BB v. Ministry of Health of the Republic of Lithuania*, C-166/20, ECLI:EU:C:2021:554.

60 SACL, Decision of 5 January 2022 in administrative case No. eA-694-822/2021.

II. Definition of the Rule of Law from a Lithuanian Perspective

In the Preamble of the Constitution of Lithuania, the striving for an open, just, and harmonious civil society and state under the rule of law is established. In its ruling of 14 March 2006, the Constitutional Court noted that the constitutional principle of the rule of law obliges the institutions applying the law not to deviate from the general principles of law enshrined in the jurisprudence of democratic legal states.

The Constitutional Court maintains that the constitutional principle of the rule of law is a universal principle upon which the entire Lithuanian legal system and the Constitution itself are founded. It needs to be noted that the constitutional principle of a state under the rule of law is a universal one upon which the whole Lithuanian legal system as well as the Constitution of the Republic of Lithuania itself are based and that the content of the principle of a state under the rule of law can be detected in various provisions of the Constitution and should be construed inseparably from the striving for an open, just, and harmonious civil society and state under the rule of law declared in the Preamble of the Constitution. Along with the other requirements, the principle of a state under the rule of law consolidated in the Constitution also pre-supposes the fact that human rights and freedoms must be ensured (Constitutional Court ruling, 23 February 2000).

The substance of this constitutional principle is articulated through various provisions of the Constitution. The core of this principle lies in the supremacy of law. The constitutional principle of the rule of law is broad and encompassing, incorporating a range of interconnected imperatives (Constitutional Court ruling, 3 July 2012). *E. Kūris* categorizes the constitutional principle of the rule of law as a coordinating principle[61], observing that various facets of the rule of law, as a comprehensive constitutional idea, are reflected in numerous provisions of the Constitution. These include the

61 According to *Kūris*, the coordinating principles determine the regulation set out in the Constitution itself, determining how one constitutional norm fits in with the others and with the principles enshrined in the Constitution. They coordinate the constitutional regulation itself. This refers to the way in which consistency in the content of constitutional regulation is ensured. If a legal regulation is contrary to the Constitution (any of its provisions), it "automatically" violates a coordinating principle, *Kūris*, On the Rule of Law and the Quality of the Law: Reflections of the Constitutional-Turned International Judge, in: Teoría y realidad constitucional núm. 42.

provision that the Lithuanian state is an independent democratic republic (Article 1), the stipulation that governmental powers are limited by the Constitution (Article 5 (2)), the assertion that the Constitution is a unified and directly applicable legal act (Article 6 (1)), the provision that no law or other act contrary to the Constitution shall have legal force (Article 7 (1)), and the principle that only promulgated laws are valid (Article 7 (2)). Further, it is reflected in the recognition that human rights and freedoms are inalienable (Article 18), as well as in provisions ensuring the independence of judges and courts and safeguarding fundamental human rights such as the right to life, dignity, and the inviolability of private life, among others[62].

III. The Right to an Effective Judicial Remedy as an Essential Requirement of the Rule of Law

There is no doubt that the right to an effective judicial remedy is an essential element of realising the rule of law. The importance of access to justice in the context of the rule of law is aptly described by the ECHR in one of its fundamental judgments in the case of *Golder v. the United Kingdom* – one can scarcely conceive of the rule of law without there being a possibility of having access to the courts[63]. The ECHR has repeatedly pointed out that Article 6(1) of the Convention on Human Rights establishes the „right to a trial", of which the right to initiate legal proceedings is only one of the aspects. However, that aspect essentially determines whether the person concerned will be able to avail himself of the other guarantees provided for in Article 6(1) of the Convention.

The right to an effective remedy is an essential requirement of ensuring the rule of law (Article 2 TEU) within the Union. The right to an effective judicial remedy is a general principle of EU law. It is linked to obligations in Article 19(1) TEU under which European courts shall ensure that in the interpretation and application of the Treaties the law is observed. Under the same article, Member States shall through their national courts provide remedies sufficient to ensure effective legal protection in the fields covered by Union law.

---

62 Kūris, Lietuvos Respublikos Konstitucijos principai//Lietuvos konstitucinė teisė, 2001, p. 235-254.

63 ECHR, *Golder v. the United Kingdom* (21.2.1975), App. no. 4451/70.

The CJEU has also confirmed that access to justice is an integral part of the legal community and is guaranteed by the legal order based on the TEU, which has established a comprehensive system of remedies and procedures to enable the CJEU to review the legality of acts adopted by the institutions[64].

The CJEU has summarised this in *Trade Union of Portuguese Judges* by stating that the European Union is a union based on the rule of law in which individual parties have the right to challenge before the courts the legality of any decision or other national measure relating to the application to them of an EU act[65]. Article 19 TEU, in this context, gives concrete expression to the value of the rule of law stated in Article 2 TEU, entrusts the responsibility for ensuring judicial review in the EU legal order not only to the Court of Justice but also to national courts and tribunals. Therefore, as the CJEU now has repeatedly underlined, the very existence of effective judicial review designed to ensure compliance with EU law is of the essence of the rule of law[66].

The principle of effective judicial protection is also enshrined in Article 47 of the Charter[67]. The CJEU affirms that the right to an effective remedy, as guaranteed by Article 47 of the Charter, entails, among other elements, the right of individuals to access a judicial body competent to uphold rights established by EU law and to assess and resolve all factual and legal issues relevant to the case[68]. It is discussed whether Member State obligations arising from Article 19 (1) TEU, which speaks of the "fields covered" by EU law, may require a broader reading than the notion of 'scope' or 'implementation' of EU law which defines the scope of application

---

64 ECJ, *Les Verts v. Parliament*, C-294/83, ECLI:EU:C:1986:166, p. 23.

65 ECJ, *Associação Sindical dos Juízes Portugueses*, C-64/16, ECLI:EU:C:2018:117, para. 31.

66 *Hofmann*, A Commentary on the right to an effective remedy in the case law of the CJEU, University of Luxembourg Law Working Paper No. 2019-016, available at: https://papers.ssrn.com/sol3/papers.cfm?abstract_id=3503540 (last access: 23.10.2025).

67 ECJ, *DEB Deutsche Energiehandels- und Beratungsgesellschaft mbH v. Bundesrepublik Deutschland*, C-279/09, ECLI:EU:C:2010:811, p. 30 and 31.

68 In this regard, see ECJ, *Otis and others*, C-199/11, ECLI:EU:C:2012:684, para. 49, and *Aktiva Finants*, C-433/18, ECLI:EU:C:2019:1074, p. 36.

of EU general principles of law to Member States or under Article 51 CFR, defining the scope of application of the Charter including Article 47 CFR[69].

There are also several examples where a national court has been confronted with a possible restriction of the right to an effective judicial remedy. In one of the cases, the Supreme Administrative Court of Lithuania reviewed the restriction on the disposal of the applicants' funds frozen under the restrictive measures imposed on Belarus in order to implement the applicants' right to a judicial remedy (payment of professional fees and reimbursement of legal expenses)[70].

In the present case, the dispute arose as to the legality and reasonableness of the decisions of the Ministry of Foreign Affairs, as well as of the decisions of the Financial Crime Investigation Service refusing to grant the applicants' requests for authorisation to use a part of the frozen funds for the purpose of payment of the costs of legal aid, and the defendants' duty to re-examine the applicants' requests. The Court of First Instance partially upheld the applicants' complaint and instructed the defendants to reassess the applicants' submissions, concluding that the contested legal acts fail to comply with the provisions of the Law on Public Administration, as they lack a basis in objective data and the refusal to act is unsubstantiated.

By its ruling of 3 May 2013, the Supreme Administrative Court of Lithuania submitted a request for a preliminary ruling to the CJEU regarding the interpretation of the Council Regulation (EC) No. 765/2006 on restrictive measures against Belarus. In response to this request, the CJEU clarified[71] that, under the relevant provisions of Council Regulation (EC) No. 765/2006, the competent national authority does not possess absolute discretion when assessing a request for an exception under this regulation to initiate proceedings challenging the legality of restrictive measures imposed by the EU. Instead, it must exercise its powers in accordance with the rights enshrined in the second sentence of the second paragraph of Article 47 of the Charter and ensure compliance with the requirement that the applicant be represented by a lawyer when bringing an action before the court. The CJEU also held that the competent national authority is entitled to verify that the funds subject to a freezing request are allocated exclusively for the payment of reasonable professional fees and the reimbursement of expenses

69 *Prechal*, Article 19 TEU And National Courts: A New Role For The Principle Of Effective Judicial Protection?, *REALaw.blog*, 29.11.2022, available at: https://wp.me/pcQ0x2-wL (last access: 23.10.2025).

70 SACL, Ruling of 3 Mai 2013, No. A[858]-283/2013.

71 ECJ, *Peftiev and others*, C-314/13, ECLI:EU:C:2014:1645.

incurred in connection with the provision of legal services. Additionally, it may impose any conditions it considers appropriate to ensure that the objective of the imposed sanction is upheld and that the granted exemption is not misused.

The Supreme Administrative Court, considering the clarifications provided in the preliminary ruling, observed that the requirements regarding the content of an administrative act – specifically, the obligation to indicate the reasons for its adoption – encompass both substantive and procedural aspects. These requirements are intrinsically linked to an individual's right to judicial protection. In this context, it is important to note that an administrative act lacking procedural justification and adversely affecting the rights or interests of an individual cannot be deemed lawful, as it restricts the subject's right to challenge the act and hinders effective judicial review. This stands in direct contradiction to an individual's right to judicial protection, including due process and a fair hearing, as enshrined in Article 6 of the European Convention on Human Rights. Failure to correlate specific legal norms with objective data (facts) must be regarded as a fundamental deficiency. Such a violation not only infringes upon an individual's right to be informed of the scope of an unlawful act and restricts access to judicial protection but also, when the dispute is brought before the court, prevents the judiciary from fully comprehending and defining the scope of the case, thereby hindering a comprehensive and objective examination of the dispute[72].

Under these circumstances, the Supreme Administrative Court of Lithuania ruled that the reasoning provided was inadequate and flawed, constituting a fundamental violation. This deficiency served as an independent ground for annulling the contested acts as unlawful.

In another case reviewed by national courts, concerning violations of the right to judicial protection, border procedures were applied to foreigners who crossed the Lithuanian border unlawfully, leading to their formal classification as not having been admitted to the Republic of Lithuania.

Under the legal framework established by the Law on the Legal Status of Aliens, a foreigner could be placed under an accommodation measure that restricted their freedom of movement within Lithuania for up to six months, without a clearly defined mechanism for legally verifying the legitimacy of such a measure. The Supreme Administrative Court in such

72 SACL, Judgment of 23 September 2014, No. A^{858}-47/2014.

cases[73], reversed the lower court's decisions rejecting foreign nationals' applications for alternative detention measures. Most of the applications were rejected on the grounds that the foreigners were not considered to be in detention.

The cases under review underscored that, in accordance with both the Constitution and international law, the applicants must be effectively guaranteed the right to judicial protection to assess the validity and legality of the measures imposed on them – specifically, accommodation without the right to free movement within the territory of the Republic of Lithuania. The declaration of a state of emergency does not serve as a valid justification for restricting this right to defense. As stipulated in Article 145 of the Constitution, the right to access the courts cannot be temporarily suspended, even in the event of a state of war or emergency.

In one of the cases concerning the *de facto* detention of a third-country national who had illegally entered the territory of Lithuania, the Supreme Administrative Court referred to the CJEU for a preliminary ruling on whether EU law prohibited a national legal regulation which, in the context of an emergency situation resulting from a mass influx of foreigners, prevents a person who has illegally entered the territory of Lithuania from lodging an application for international protection and by which an asylum seeker may be detained solely on the ground that he or she has entered the territory of Lithuania by illegally crossing the border[74].

After the CJEU, in its judgment in *M.A.*[75] had clarified that such rules of national law are prohibited by Directives 2013/32/EU and 2013/33/EU of the European Parliament and of the Council[76], the Supreme Administrative Court upheld the rights of the third-country national by finding that he should have been considered an asylum seeker[77].

It is crucial to emphasize that the Constitutional Court, in its ruling of 7 June 2023, determined that a provision of the Law on the Legal Status of Aliens, which required asylum seekers to be accommodated in designated

73 See SACL, Ruling of 6 October 2021, No. AS-653-492/2021, Ruling of 3 November 2021, No. A-4071-492/2021, Ruling of 18 November 2021, No. A-4180-629/2021.

74 SACL, Ruling of 2 February 2022, No. A-1091-822/2022.

75 ECJ, *Valstybės sienos apsaugos tarnyba*, C-72/22 PPU, ECLI:EU:C:2022:505.

76 Directive 2013/32/EU of the European Parliament and of the Council of 26 June 2013 on common procedures for granting and withdrawing international protection, OJ 2013 L 180, p. 60, and Directive 2013/33/EU of the European Parliament and of the Council of 26 June 2013 laying down standards for the reception of applicants for international protection (recast), OJ 2013 L 180, p. 96.

77 SACL, Judgment of 28 July 2022, No. A-1091-822/2022.

locations without granting them the right to free movement within the Republic of Lithuania, in the event of a mass influx of aliens during a declared emergency, state of emergency, or state of war, violated Article 20 of the Constitution. This provision mandated that such accommodation could last up to six months without a decision by the competent institution that could be appealed to the courts. The Constitutional Court found this measure problematic, as it imposed one of the most restrictive forms of personal liberty on all asylum seekers without individually assessing each person's situation or the real threat, they might pose to the values protected by the Constitution, or to the state's and society's interests. Additionally, the Constitutional Court noted that there was no opportunity for judicial review of the legality or justification of such measures, which was compounded by the lack of provision for alternative, less restrictive measures to safeguard personal freedom.

During the migration crisis in Lithuania, challenges concerning the protection of human rights were unavoidable in areas such as the admissibility of international protection applications, the granting of asylum seeker status, the grounds, terms, and conditions of *de facto* detention, as well as decisions on the granting or denial of such protection. In this context, the courts played a crucial role in balancing competing values. The referral by the Supreme Administrative Court to the CJEU, seeking a preliminary ruling on the provisions of directives concerning the restriction of the right to apply for international protection and the detention of asylum seekers during a state of emergency, as well as the ECHR decision to apply interim measures – ordering Lithuania not to expel aliens who are already on its territory – are just a few examples of numerous cases that national courts in Lithuania and other EU border states with Belarus had to address, testing the interpretation of EU regulations, including those enshrined in the Charter.

The Supreme Administrative Court set a comprehensive standard for evaluating the legality and justification of restrictions on freedom, involving a detailed, case-by-case analysis of both factual and legal circumstances. This evaluation must take into account not only national legal provisions but also international and EU law, alongside the practices of the ECHR and CJEU. National legal provisions, which did not offer the possibility to appeal accommodation measures, did not prevent the Supreme Administrative Court of Lithuania from establishing the requirement for judicial review of the justification and legality of restrictions on the fundamental human right to freedom of movement. This clearly shows that the crisis situation itself was not a reason to weaken or change the interpretation of the sufficiently strict human rights protection standards previously developed in the practices of the CJEU, ECHR, and national courts.

The Constitutional Court also emphasizes the importance of strictly following this standard. In the previously mentioned ruling of 7 June 2023, regarding the legality of national regulations concerning the automatic detention of incoming foreigners, the Constitutional Court applied the proportionality test consistently developed in the case law of the ECHR, CJEU, and its own doctrine. The legal framework governing the detention of foreigners must be clear, accessible, predictable, and include an obligation for authorities to apply detention in accordance with the principles of necessity and proportionality, making reasoned written decisions and ensuring effective procedural guarantees, including the right to appeal to the courts.

Recently, in cases handled by the Supreme Administrative Court, new issues have come up, especially regarding the assessment of national security threats posed by foreign nationals. In these cases, there was a risk that the right to effective judicial remedies would become purely declaratory. With Russia's invasion of Ukraine in 2022, the position of foreigners on the aggression against Ukraine has become a key factor in determining an individual's potential threat to national security. However, this does not lead to an automatic threat assessment. Lithuanian court practice shows that, even under these circumstances, the evaluation of each specific case remains essential. The application of the proportionality test in such situations means that a foreign national's long-term resident status cannot be revoked or denied simply because the State Security Department's report claims the individual poses a security threat. The threat to national security must not be assumed automatically; decisions must be based on a careful analysis of the facts and circumstances to prevent unjustified human rights restrictions.

In conclusion, finding a balance between national interests, national security, and human rights protection remains a key issue during various crises affecting the European community. In this effort, attention is drawn to the core values and principles outlined in Article 2 of the TEU.

IV. The Right to Privacy and the Rule of Law

Another practice demonstrating the harmony and complementarity of the provisions of the Constitution and EU law, including the principle of the rule of law, relates to the protection of the right to privacy in the interpretation of the concept of family and in other cases.

Article 7 of the Charter enshrines the right to respect for family life. It has to be interpreted and applied together with the right to marry and the right to establish a family, which is provided in Article 9 of the Charter (as well as the corresponding provisions of Articles 8 and 12 of the ECHR). A sufficiently high standard for the protection of these individual rights is established. Although family law is a sensitive area under EU law, Member States have some discretion in deciding how to ensure the right to respect for family life.

However, both the gender-neutral provision of Article 9 of the Charter, which grants the right to marry, and the case law of the CJEU, based on ECHR human rights standards, show that the European standard of the right to respect for family life is evolving towards the recognition of the legal status of same-sex couples. However, although Lithuanian law is not effective in relation to civil partnerships, Lithuanian courts rely on EU provisions in this respect and seek to ensure fundamental rights based on international standards, including the rule of law.

By annulling the competent institution's refusal to issue a residence permit to a third-country national seeking family reunification with an EU Member State citizen in a same-sex marriage, the Supreme Administrative Court of Lithuania[78] applied the interpretation provided by the Constitutional Court in the relevant case. This interpretation underscored that, under EU law, a Member State cannot invoke a public policy exception – such as the absence of same-sex marriage recognition in its national legislation – to deny family reunification between an EU citizen (including its own nationals) who has exercised her freedom of movement and a third-country national of the same sex who has lawfully entered into marriage in another Member State. In this case, even though Lithuanian national law does not recognize same-sex marriages or partnerships, the Supreme Administrative Court prioritized the protection of individuals' right to privacy. It was held that the refusal to issue the residence permit in question could not be justified solely on the basis of the foreign national's gender identity

78 SACL, Ruling of 20 March 2019, No. eA-3227-624/2019.

and/or sexual orientation. Accordingly, the legal framework was assessed and adapted, considering not only the domestic legal context but also the broader social and legal landscape across other EU Member States.

In the context of the right to private life, the decision of the Extended Chamber of Judges of the Supreme Administrative Court[79] irative case is also relevant[80]. The Court examined the legality of the Hygiene Standard approved by the Minister of Health, as well as the rules for completing the Child Health Certificate, following a request submitted by members of the Parliament.

The provision of the Hygienic Standard under examination established that, in the absence of medical contraindications, a child who had not been vaccinated against the specified diseases in accordance with the approved Children's Preventive Immunization Calendar would not be admitted to the pre-primary education programme. Additionally, the rules governing the completion of the child's health certificate required that, for children enrolled in pre-school and/or pre-primary education institutions, the certificate must indicate whether they had received all mandatory vaccinations for attendance.

In its ruling, the Supreme Administrative Court of Lithuania held that the prohibition on admitting unvaccinated children to educational institutions, as a restriction on the right to body integrity – an integral aspect of an individual's right to private life – must be established by law. Consequently, the contested provisions of the Hygienic Standard and the rules for completing the Child Health Certificate were found to be inconsistent with the principle of the hierarchy of legal acts, which is enshrined in the constitutional principle of the rule of law.

The right to privacy is closely linked to the right to access information, which is guaranteed by Article 10 of the ECHR. In the context of European Union law, access to information first of all has the status of a common constitutional tradition, secondly a right of freedom of expression and information, including the freedom to hold opinions and to receive and impart information and ideas without interference by public authority and regardless of frontiers, is laid down in Article 11 of the Charter.

A special role in ensuring the right to personal data protection and the freedom of information rests with national courts: dealing with the relevant

---

79 SACL, Judgment of 20 March 2019, No. eA-3227-624/2019.
80 SACL, Judgment of 5 July 2016, No I-6-662/2016.

cases, they have to assess, where necessary, if the fundamental rights is not breached.

The important issue is how international and national courts balance the right to personal data protection and the freedom of information. The right to information and the right to personal data protection or privacy are both internationally recognized human rights with a long history and important functions. According to the human rights law, no right is typically accorded a greater weight in comparison to another. The rights must be analysed on a case-by-case basis paying attention to relative importance of various interests.

In many cases the Supreme Administrative Court has given priority to the freedom of information by expanding the interpretation of information processing for business purposes. On the other hand, the SACL also focuses on the fact that personal data may be processed for a legitimate purpose only and in that case identifying a certain legitimate purpose from the data controllers' point of view is not sufficient; normally, the SACL carries out the proportionality test provided for in the jurisprudence of the ECHR and the CJEU.

The Supreme Administrative Court, when examining a dispute concerning the decision of the Inspector of Journalist Ethics in relation to several publications containing information about a person on the list of the Lithuanian richest people and the list of the Lithuanian richest women, ruled on the right of the public to be informed about the richest persons in Lithuania. In the present case, when ranking a person on the basis of the value of his assets, the article contained the person's name, surname, photograph, marital status, age, place of birth and place of residence[81]. When assessing the classification of the richest persons as public persons, the SACL emphasised that the concept of a public person should be interpreted in the light of the ECHR case-law, and pointed out that the country's richest persons occupy such a position in society, that it makes their activities related to the management of their assets relevant to public affairs (creation of many jobs, business environment, collection of taxes to the state budget), and, therefore, they are public persons within the meaning of both the Convention on the Protection of Human Rights and Fundamental Freedoms and the domestic law.

---

81 SACL, Judgment of 15 September 2021 in administrative case No eA-2066-624/2021.

D. Coclusions

Undoubtedly, the common legal values create mutual trust between the Member States, and also bring them together for common action. There is a fundamental reason that Paragraph 1 of the Preamble to the Charter declares that the peoples of Europe, in creating an ever closer union among them, are resolved to share a peaceful future based on common values.

The rule of law and the protection of fundamental rights have always played a central role within the process of European integration, and today, have acquired an increasing normative value in the EU legal system. The rule of law, as a fundamental principle common to the EU legal system, closely relates with the protection of human rights. The primacy of the rule of law in democratic societies has been firmly recognized, reinforcing the need to uphold justice. As a foundational principle, it requires respect for the separation of powers and the provision of access to an independent judiciary.

However, a fair resolution of disputes is only possible if the balance between the fundamental values underpinning the EU and the national legal systems of the Member States, as set out in Article 2 TEU, is maintained. In resolving disputes, Lithuanian courts have consistently emphasised the synthesis of the constitutional provisions and the legal system of the European Union, the common value context, and the complementarity of each other, as both the law of the European Union and the Constitution are based on the principles of democracy, respect for fundamental human rights and other values.

The rule of law is generally understood as a principle that includes substantive components (e.g. equality before the law) as well as formal procedural elements (e.g. legal certainty, judicial review), and which requires a democratic and liberal constitutional order giving full effect to human rights.

The Lithuanian legal system demonstrates a successful model of constitutional pluralism, wherein EU law and the national constitution coexist harmoniously through what scholars call "friendly two-way interpretation". This approach allows Lithuanian courts to uphold both constitutional sovereignty and EU legal obligations without sacrificing the protection of fundamental rights. As evidenced by cases involving family reunification, asylum procedures, and data protection, Lithuanian courts consistently interpret domestic legislation in light of EU law and international human rights standards, thereby strengthening the rule of law in practice rather than merely in theory.

The principle of effective judicial remedy serves as a cornerstone of the rule of law in Lithuania's legal practice. Even during emergency situations, such as the migration crisis or security concerns related to Russia's aggression against Ukraine, Lithuanian courts have maintained strict adherence to the standards developed by the CJEU and ECHR. The case law reveals that national courts perform crucial functions in ensuring that restrictions on fundamental rights undergo rigorous scrutiny through proportionality tests and individualized assessments, preventing arbitrary limitations on human rights even when national security interests are at stake.

The implementation of the rule of law in Lithuanian jurisprudence confirms the intrinsic connection between rule of law and human rights protection. Far from being competing principles, the two concepts are mutually reinforcing in practice. This is particularly evident in cases concerning privacy rights, family life, and detention of migrants, where courts apply comprehensive legal frameworks that draw upon constitutional values, EU law, and international human rights standards. The Lithuanian experience demonstrates that effective implementation of rule of law principles serves to strengthen human rights protections, confirming the theoretical position that substantive conceptions of the rule of law inherently encompass respect for fundamental rights.

Missing Links? The EU, Democracy and the Public

Sven Simon

At a time when Europe's political path faces many contingencies, it is important to engage with questions of the democratic functioning of the European Union. A starting point in examining these questions is offered through the rulings of the German Constitutional Court (hereinafter – BVerfG) on European integration and the role of democracy. The German Grundgesetz (hereinafter – GG) in Art. 23 par. 1 states, with a view to establishing a united Europe, that the Federal Republic of Germany shall participate in the development of the European Union that is committed to democratic principles. This kind of constitutional provision is comparatively unusual, but compels the German institutions to address the issue of the democratic legitimacy of EU activities. This paper features previous research[1] on European democracy as well as practical insights as a lawmaker in the European Parliament throughout the past five years.

A. Setting the scene: supranational democracy in Europe

The democratic legitimacy of the European Union consists of two strands: firstly, it is a "*union among the peoples of Europe*" (Art. 1 para. 2 TEU) and is based on the peoples that make up the Member States.[2] At European level, the peoples of Europe act through their governments, which derive their democratic legitimacy in accordance with the legal principles and traditions of the respective Member State. The European Parliament, as a representative body elected directly by the citizens of the EU, forms the second strand of democratic legitimacy.

1 *Simon*, Grenzen des Bundesverfassungsgerichts im europäischen Integrationsprozess, 2016, p. 164-212.

2 For a more detailed analysis, see, among others, *von Achenbach*, Zum Prinzip dualer demokratischer Legitimation supranationaler Herrschaft – Vorschlag einer Demokratietheorie des Verhältnisses von Europäischem Parlament und Rat, in: Vöneky (ed.), Informationspapiere der Max-Planck-Forschungsgruppe „Demokratische Legitimation ethischer Entscheidungen", 2/2008, pp. 2 et seq.

Under Art. 10 TEU, the functioning of the European Union is based on representative democracy. Hence, European citizens have the right to directly elect the European Parliament. The Member States, meanwhile, are represented in the European Council by their Heads of State or Government and in the Council by their governments, themselves democratically accountable either to their national parliaments or to their citizens. Insofar as the Union has competences conferred on it, this is the mechanism by which its decisions are democratically legitimised. Democratic legitimacy therefore flows from the primary political realm of the Member States, their parliaments and elected governments and the independent source of legitimacy provided by the directly elected European Parliament.[3]

B. Criticism of the European model of democracy

However, this ideal type of European democracy has faced critiques in the past. It is widely held that the first strand of legitimacy in the form of the Council of the European Union is not fully consistent with the principle of democracy, since it is based on a derivative source of legitimacy, not an original one.[4] Moreover, when the Council legislates, there is no political cleavage, as there is in national parliaments. Rather, there is a negotiation between different national interests.[5] Furthermore, the Union's laws can be passed (at least in some cases) without a majority in the European Parliament,[6] and that Parliament has not as yet been granted any (formal) right to initiate legislation.[7] Members of the European Parliament are not

3 *Di Fabio*, Der Auftrag zur europäischen Integration und seine Grenzen, in: Ruffert (ed.), Dynamik und Nachhaltigkeit des Öffentlichen Rechts, Festschrift für Reinhardt Schröder, 2012, p. 169 (174); *Schröder*, Die Parlamente im europäischen Entscheidungsgefüge, EuR 2002, 301 (315).

4 Cf. BVerfGE 89, 155 (182 et seq.) (Maastricht); *P. Kirchhof*, Der deutsche Staat in der europäischen Integration, in: HStR X, 2012 (3rd edition), § 214, recital 102.

5 *Grimm*, Die Rolle der nationalen Verfassungsgerichte in der europäischen Demokratie, in: Franzius/Mayer/Neyer (eds.), Grenzen der europäischen Integration. Herausforderung für Recht und Politik, 2014, p. 27 (30).

6 This is seldom relevant in practice, cf. *Lehne/Freudenberg*, Tendenz zur gesetzgeberischen Übertreibung, ZRP 2013, 58 (59).

7 The European Parliament successfully argued for a de facto right to initiate legislation under Art. 225 TFEU through the revision of the Framework Agreement on relations between the European Parliament and the European Commission signed on 20.10.2010.

elected under a system in which all votes have equal weight (Art. 14 para. 3 TEU), but as a function of national contingents (Art. 14 para. 2 TEU).

This critique emphasizes also that the "*pre-legal requirements for a democracy*"[8] have not yet developed. This is a reference to "the constant free debate between social forces, interests and ideas as they come into contact with one another, for which the parties, organisations, press and broadcasting organisations operating across Europe serve as a medium and a factor in a process of dissemination."[9] *Udo di Fabio* describes the problem by posing the question of where Europe actually governs from, where the *volonté générale* that supposedly forms the foundation of the idea of democracy in being ascribed to the "*will of the people*" is shaped.[10]

It is Karlsruhe's view that democracy, "*if it is to be more than a purely formal principle of apportionment, depends upon the fulfilment of certain pre-legal prerequisites, such as an ongoing, free debate between social powers, interests and ideas as they come into contact with one another, wherein political goals are also clarified and transformed*[11] *and through which public opinion moulds the political will.*"[12] The German Federal Constitutional Court has repeatedly "refined" its criticism of the European Union's democratic model. Firstly, there was the lack of a directly elected parliament, then the lack of an equal division of powers between Parliament and the Council, and finally the problem of deficiencies in electoral equality. Thus, the Court looks for the source of the democratic deficit in the EU primarily at institutional level.

The European Parliament takes centre stage in the Federal Constitutional Court's consideration of the democratic deficit in the European Union.[13] The Court comes to the conclusion that even after the reformulation of Art. 14 para. 2 TEU under the Lisbon Treaty, the European Parliament is "*not a body representing a sovereign European people*".[14] Because of

8 BVerfGE 89, 155 (185) (Maastricht); *P. Kirchhof* (fn. 4), § 214, recital 102.

9 *P. Kirchhof*, Der deutsche Staat in der europäischen Integration, HStR X, 2012 (3rd edition), § 214, recital 102.

10 *Di Fabio*, „Mehrebenendemokratie in Europa", lecture at the Humboldt-Universität zu Berlin on 15.11.2001 (FCE 10/01), p. 1.

11 Cf. BVerfGE 5, 85 (135, 198, 205) (KPD ban); 69, 315 (344 et seq.) (Brokdorf).

12 BVerfGE 89, 155 (185) (Maastricht).

13 On this note, see: *Gerhardt*, Europäisches Parlament und Bundesverfassungsgericht, NVwZ-Beilage 2013, 53 et seq.

14 BVerfGE 123, 267 (372) (Lissabon); *Kottmann/Wohlfahrt*, Der gespaltene Wächter? Demokratie, Verfassungsidentität und Integrationsverantwortung im *Lissabon*-Urteil, ZaöRV 2009, 443 (452).

its structure based on national contingents of Members of the European Parliament, the Court maintains that the European Parliament remains a body representing the peoples (of the Member States). The view of the Court is that it continues to have a merely complementary rather than the central role in legitimising European sovereignty. With the current arrangements for elections to the European Parliament, it does not meet the criteria set by the Federal Constitutional Court. The Second Senate of the Constitutional Court refuses to accept that, for practical and political reasons, there is no alternative to the unequal weighting of votes. The Court also rejects the expectation that greater involvement of national parliaments could significantly improve the degree of democratic legitimacy. One could discuss at length the merits of the Federal Constitutional Court's arguments and how the provisions of Art. 23 of the German constitution are to be weighed against them. In my habilitation, I concluded that the Federal Constitutional Court paints an idealised picture of a parliamentary democracy which will not be achievable, practical or indeed desirable for the European level.[15] With a view to the Bundesrat, it is even doubtful, whether the democratic nature of the Federal Republic of Germany, as a federal state, matches the standards of democracy characterised by egalitarian majority rule as set out by the Federal Constitutional Court.

C. Material democratic deficit

However, it is promising to focus instead on the material democratic deficits of the European level. Regardless of how representative institutions are elected in a democracy, whether a polity is also democratic in a material sense hinges on a number of other conditions. The institutional argument concerning the inadequately democratic make-up of the European Union must be distinguished from the material democratic deficit.

Given the challenges of modern statehood and the associated changes to the interpretation of the democratic principle in Art. 20 para. 2 GG, *Niels Petersen* brought the "*deliberative democratic model*"[16] to the table.

15 *Simon* (fn. 1), p. 211.

16 Introduction and overview following, for instance, *Dryzek*, Discursive Democracy, 1990; the seminal work is *Habermas*, Faktizität und Geltung. Beiträge zur Diskurstheorie des Rechts und des demokratischen Rechtsstaats, 1992, p. 349 et seq. For the theory, see also *Fishkin*, Democracy and Deliberation: New Directions for Democrat-

Here he assumes four criteria which he says can be "*derived from theoretical considerations about the scrutiny and epistemic quality of political processes*".[17] He considers these criteria to be *accountability, deliberation, pluralism and expertise.* Firstly, he writes, it must be ensured that the political decision-makers are subject to adequate *accountability* so that they act in the public interest. Furthermore, decision-making mechanisms are to be designed so that they are as deliberative as possible, both internally and externally. Internal *deliberation* must take place within decision-making bodies. Above all, therefore, those institutions in which important decisions are made must be "*designed as far as possible as non-hierarchical, collegiate bodies, so that every decision can be preceded by a debate*". By external *deliberation,* he means discussion with the general public or with an expert audience. An example of the latter might be the scholarly discourse on jurisprudence which in part prepares the way for court decisions, and in part reviews it after the fact. He names *pluralism* as another central element. Where membership of collective institutions is skewed too far in one direction, he writes, this often leads to greater polarisation of decisions, which undermines their quality. In particular, a greater degree of *pluralism* can be achieved if different social groups are allowed to present their points of view in certain decision-making processes without them being granted formal decision-making powers. Finally, the fourth element of his theory is *expertise.* Many differences of opinion, in his view, stem from a "*lack of awareness of the facts, so that the quality of decisions is directly improved by* expertise [emphasis by the author]." This can be introduced by delegating decisions, at least in part, to groups of experts, or by consulting such groups. In this context, multiphase decision-making processes, where decisions are prepared by experts and then discussed and adopted in public forums, are especially promising.[18] *Petersen* sees these criteria as an imperative for optimisation. Applying *Petersen's* model and utilizing my personal experience in the Parliament over the past five years one can identify

ic Reform, 1991; *Ferejohn*, Instituting Deliberative Democracy, in: Shapiro/Macedo (eds.), Designing Democratic Institutions, 2000, p. 75.

17 *Petersen*, Demokratie und Grundgesetz: Veränderungen des Demokratieprinzips in Art. 20 Abs. 2 GG angesichts der Herausforderungen Moderner Staatlichkeit, JöR 58 (2010), p. 137 (169).

18 For a more detailed conception of the legislative process in the European Union, see *Petersen*, The Democracy Concept of the European Union – Coherent Constitutional Principle or Prosaic Declaration of Intent?, in: Dann/Rynkowski (eds.), The Unity of the European Constitution, 2006, p. 97 (115).

several material democratic deficits or rather missing links in democratic legitimacy:

I. National fragmentation of political discourse

Firstly, the European Union is subject to profound national fragmentation. Institutionally, "*the value of European integration is predominantly measured against the benefits for one's own country.*"[19] Compounding this, the parties that form public opinion act primarily and almost exclusively at national level. They conduct their electoral campaigns largely independently and focus on national topics. While Members with similar fundamental convictions do subsequently form groups in Parliament, these groups are not rooted in social cleavages, nor are citizens aware of them as political parties. Their joint voting record in Parliament is often delegation-bound. They have virtually no public role in the political decision-making process. Political contestation thus continues to take place primarily at the national level. As a result, European party groupings "*cannot perform their mediating role between EU citizens and the EU institutions, because they are not connected with the electorate and cannot be held accountable by them, whereas national parties cannot convincingly promise that the platform on which they campaign will be taken up by the group in the European Parliament after the election.*"[20]

II. Lack of an inner-parliamentary public

This national fragmentation is not merely an outside problem, but also a problem for the functioning of the Parliament within. The 705 Members of the European Parliament currently represent over 200 different national political parties. This fragmentation has consequences for the political groups as a space for deliberation. In parliamentary practice, Members are allocated between 60 and 120 seconds of speaking time in plenary. As a consequence, debates within the house consist of the consecutive reading of pre-prepared statements instead of a real debate in which speakers engage in substance with each other. This does not only reduce the attractiveness

19 *Grimm*, Die Stärke der EU liegt in einer klugen Begrenzung, Frankfurter Allgemeine Zeitung, 11.8.2014, p. 11.
20 *Ibid.*

of said debates to the wider public but prevents an effective exchange of arguments.

III. Different national traditions of a free mandate

The current European electoral law from 1976 does not specify obligations for Member States on how to elect their Members for the European Parliament, except for the requirement of a proportional system. Unlike some electoral laws in Member States, such as in Germany, there are no provisions on internal democratic structures and selection mechanisms within political parties. As a consequence in some Member States, candidates are chosen by fiat through the chairperson of the national party, often only shortly before the deadline of nomination at the end of the mandate. In Germany, party conferences select candidates and give individual aspirants the opportunity to challenge any pre-selection by the party leadership. Recognizing the inherent democratic deficit in the absence of such structures, the European Parliament in 2022 made a proposal to revise the European electoral law and incorporate norms on internal democracy into Union law. However, no progress has since been made in Council towards its adoption, and the next European Parliament will still be elected using the 1976 law. This has substantial consequences for the voting behaviour of colleagues as it creates a strong dependence on their national party leadership. Anecdotally I can share an experience of having to call a national Prime Minister in order to get his green light for the support of his national delegation in my group ahead of an important vote, the delegation itself would not act independently. This raises questions of whether the different strands of legitimacy between order-bound Council members and some national delegations in Parliament are so different in practice.

IV. Distorting powers of the rapporteur

In its procedures, the European Parliament uses a rapporteurship system in which a competent committee appoints an individual Member as rapporteur for a specific dossier. In legislative files, the rapporteur is responsible for drafting the committee's initial position and this report is used as a basis for amendments by other groups. Once a report has passed the plenary stage and Parliament enters inter-institutional negotiations with

Council, the rapporteur speaks on behalf of the entire Parliament during the trilogue. Whilst these positions need to be confirmed by majorities in committee and plenary, this pen-holder position makes rapporteur's extraordinarily powerful in legislative procedures. Since there are no standing majority-minority structures in the European Parliament, the appointment of rapporteurs for files alternates between political groups according to a point-based system. Once a group obtains the rapporteurship over a dossier, it is allocated internally through a call for interest. This enables Members who have a particular political interest, perhaps because of previous work as an activist in a particular field, to gain outsized influence on individual files.

V. Non-representative composition of committees

This skewing effect on the legislative output of the Parliament is compounded by varying ideological leanings of different committees, deviating from the median position of the Parliament. Unsurprisingly, the positions of the Committee on the Environment, Public Health and Food Safety were often more environmentally ambitious than those of the Committee on Industry, Research and Energy. However, this divergence creates problems for the legislative output, since the Rules of Procedure of the European Parliament allow for individual committees to enter into trilogue negotiations even before a first reading in plenary, thereby reducing the plenary to a mere confirmation vote on the overall outcome.

VI. Inadequate responsiveness of European lawmaking

Furthermore, the link back from those who are politically accountable to the will of the electorate at European level seems to be less pronounced than is generally the case at nation-state level. This is partly because the system of legitimacy is characterised by an unclear division of responsibilities — at least, as far as many citizens can tell.[21] The functions of government are divided up in subtle ways between the Commission, the

21 *P. M. Huber*, Demokratie ohne Volk oder Demokratie der Völker? – Zur Demokratiefähigkeit der Europäischen Union, in: Drexl/Kreuzer/Scheuing (eds.), Europäische Demokratie, 1999, p. 27 (55); *Kokott*, Die Staatsrechtslehre und die

Council, the European Council and Parliament. Often, it is very difficult to determine which level — national or European — was ultimately meaningfully responsible for which decision.[22] This problem could at least be alleviated, if not eliminated, through information and clarification. The way in which majorities and minorities alternate, which is seen as democratic, is a more difficult problem to address. Today's minorities — the opposition, the parties, the individual voters — expect to become tomorrow's majority, and thereby to determine the fate of the community:

> "*Majority rule, so characteristic of a democracy, is distinguished from any other form of rule in that, by its very nature, it not only requires an opposition, but recognises it politically and protects it through the principle of proportionality in the context of its basic rights and freedoms* [...]. *An imposed system of this kind must imply that the minority can always itself become the majority.*"[23]

In this sense, the European Parliament does not function as an intermediary between EU citizens and the European institutions, as is the case for the national parliaments. After a European election, citizens have the impression that everything continues as before, since there is no "regime change" and there is always a grand coalition in the Parliament. This impression does not, of course, do justice to the work of the European Parliament. *Philipp Dann* even considers the Parliament, as the "*core of the parliamentary system of the European Union, superior to* [the US] *Congress in its comparable structures*" and gives us — timidly expressed as a question — a definition of the European Parliament as a "*working parliament in the executive federalist system of the European Union*" which opens up a "*dualist option*", one which "*is in this respect very much the more promising parliamentary system compared to the one we know from the national systems of the Member States.*"[24] He is right; the voters, however, do not see it that way. In the longer term, therefore, efforts must be made to achieve

---

Veränderung ihres Gegenstandes: Konsequenzen von Europäisierung und Internationalisierung, VVDStRL 63 (2003), 7 (33).

22 *Hatje*, Demokratische Kosten souveräner Staatlichkeit im europäischen Verfassungsverbund – zu den Perspektiven der Demokratie in der Europäischen Union nach dem Urteil des Bundesverfassungsgerichts zum Vertrag von Lissabon –, EuR-Beiheft 1/2010, 123 (130).

23 *Kelsen*, Vom Wesen und Wert der Demokratie, 1981 (2nd reprint of the 2nd edition, 1929), pp. 101, 103.

24 *Dann*, Parlamente im Exekutivföderalismus, 2004, p. 406.

the goal of increasing the responsiveness of the European system.[25] Nevertheless, it cannot be ignored that at national level the idea that the daily activities of more than six million public sector workers in Germany could be managed and supervised down to the smallest detail by 17 parliaments and governments is unrealistic simply in terms of organisational theory.[26] For specific policy areas, the German Federal Constitutional Court opines that this means that there is a lack of adequate responsiveness at European level.[27] Whether the lack of an adequate link back to the will of the electorate is confined to particularly sensitive areas of policy may be an open question, but it is true that democratic legitimacy at European level must in fact be considered deficient at this present moment.

VII. Cumbersome amending of EU law

Finally, it is significantly more difficult to amend or entirely revoke a piece of legislation following a change of political direction at European level than it is at national level. Many provisions which provoke perplexity and anger in day-to-day political discussions in the Member States stem directly from the Treaties. Matters regulated at 'constitutional level' are of course not entirely removed from political control but are significantly more difficult to change. Even the outcome of elections has almost no influence on them. *Dieter Grimm* sees the fact that "*the executive and judicial institutions of the EU, the Commission and the Court of Justice*" have been "*uncoupled from democratic processes and given an independent existence, both in the Member States and in the EU itself*"[28] as the root of Europe's democracy problems. "*They reach decisions of the greatest political import in an unpolitical manner, and their own praxis makes them immune to political*

25 Cf. *Lhotta*, Integrationsverantwortung und parlamentarische Repräsentation: Ein Rückzugsgefecht – und ein Rettungsversuch, in: Lhotta/Ketelhut/Schöne (eds.), Das Lissabon-Urteil. Staat, Demokratie und europäische Integration im „verfassten politischen Primärraum", 2012, p. 67 (81 et seq.).

26 *Groß*, Grundlinien einer pluralistischen Interpretation des Demokratieprinzips, in: Redaktion Kritische Justiz (ed.), Demokratie und Grundgesetz. Eine Auseinandersetzung mit der verfassungsgerichtlichen Rechtsprechung, 2000, p. 93 (97).

27 Cf. *Schorkopf*, Die Europäische Union im Lot – Karlsruhes Rechtsspruch zum Vertrag von Lissabon, EuZW 2009, 718 (721).

28 *Grimm* (fn. 19).

redirection because of the constitutionalisation of the Treaties."[29] Far-reaching decisions are taken by means of administrative or judicial procedures without ever being discussed. Perhaps even more relevant in practice is that due to an absence of a legislative right of initiative, Parliament has little effective means of correcting legislation once an error is recognized. Individual Members are limited to petition Commissioners to start a re-cast procedure, that then is likely to take years.

D. Conclusions

Ultimately, certain deficits in democratic legitimacy at supranational level are undeniable. However, the democratic deficit has its origins less in the institutional requirements of democracy than in the current design of European polity and politics. The democratic principle sets the limits of integration at supranational level not so much in terms of competence over matters of substance as in terms of the sustainability of the mechanisms of democratic participation.[30] It will still take some time for Europe to try out various forms of democratic legitimacy. And it is true that "*the debate on how to address* [the democratic deficit of the EU – amendment by the author] *has been caught in a dichotomy that pitches EU democracy as either national or supranational.*"[31] In this context, there is indeed no "*single anchor point for the theory of democracy (...) which could in and of itself be applied as an unambiguous criterion for democracy*"[32]. Therefore, it seems convincing to "*give the democratic process itself the power to define*

29 *Ibid.*; see also *Grimm*, Die Rolle der nationalen Verfassungsgerichte in der europäischen Demokratie, in: Franzius/Mayer/Neyer (eds.), Grenzen der europäischen Integration, 2014, p. 27 (39).

30 *Nettesheim*, Wo „endet" das Grundgesetz? – Verfassungsgebung als grenzüberschreitender Prozess, Der Staat 51 (2012), 313 (331).

31 *Pittoors*, Democracy and European Union: beyond the dichotomy, Journal of European Integration, 46 (2024) 1, 127–134.

32 Worded as a question in *Möllers*, Legalität, Legitimität und Legitimation des Bundesverfassungsgerichts, in: Jestaedt/Lepsius/Möllers/C. Schönberger (eds.), Das entgrenzte Gericht [The Court Without Boundaries – translation by the author], 2011, p. 281 (336), referencing *Bryde*, Das Demokratieprinzip des Grundgesetzes als Optimierungsaufgabe, in: Redaktion Kritische Justiz (ed.), Demokratie und Grundgesetz: Eine Auseinandersetzung mit der verfassungsgerichtlichen Rechtsprechung, 2000, p. 59 (67 et seq.).

the appropriateness of particular democratic rules"[33]. Parliament itself has recognized many of these deficits and proposed to reform the Lisbon Treaty accordingly in November 2023.[34] It remains to be seen whether the Member States have a willingness to engage in such a reform process to close the missing links in the democratic functioning of the Union.

33 *Möllers* (fn. 32), p. 281 (337).

34 European Parliament, 2022/2051(INL), https://www.europarl.europa.eu/doceo/document/TA-9-2023-0427_EN.pdf (last access: 23 Oct 2025).

European Citizenship in Times of Crisis – Effects on the Implementation of Social Rights

Emilio Castorina

A. *European citizenship as the fundamental status of Member States' citizens in the "community of law"*

The establishment of European citizenship with the Maastricht Treaty (Art. 8)[1] is considered to have given origin to the construction process of a supernational socio-political area.[2] This is characterized by the shared democratic values of European constitutionalism and consequently by a common identity to be progressively strengthened through the development of a direct political bond between Member States' citizens and the European Union.

Thus, the course of integration does not follow a merely Economic trajectory[3]: the basic rights of the person have soon become part of the general principles of the communitarian law guaranteed by the Court of Justice, bringing people and States together into a single "Community of law"[4].

This communitarian concept was already present in the jurisprudence of the Court of Justice in the sixties, though it was to be enunciated more thoroughly, as we know, in the 1986 *Le Verts* Case[5], concerning the issue of violation of the principle of equality before the law by a decision taken by the Bureau of the European Parliament with regard to the economic funds meant to reimburse the costs of the political formations that partook in the 1984 European elections. Prior to that, in the well-known *Van Gend &*

1 Treaty on European Union [TEU – Maastricht Treaty], O.J. C 191/1.

2 In these terms *European Commission*, Report from the Commission on the citizenship of the Union, 21 Dec. 1993, COM (93) 702 final.

3 Opinion of Advocate General Szpunar, *Neli Valcheva v Georgios Babanarakis,* C-335/17, ECLI:EU:C:2018:242, no. 25.

4 ECJ, *Stauder*, C-29/69, ECR 1969, 00419; ECJ, *Internationale Handelsgesellschaft*, C-11/70, ECR 1970, 01125. In doctrine, see *Chiti*, Dalla «Comunità di diritto» alla Unione dei diritti, Rivista italiana di diritto pubblico comunitario, 2008.

5 ECJ, *Les Verts,* C-294/83, ECR 1986, 01339.

Loos Case[6], the European judge ruled that the States are not the only parties involved in the communitarian system since the latter provides for organs that are institutionally endowed with sovereign power they can exercise both over the Member States and their citizens.

In the *Costa Sentence* of July 15, 1964, the Court of Justice declared that the EEC Treaty established its own legal order which was accepted by the Member States on the condition of reciprocity. As a consequence, the unilateral proceedings of the Member States cannot override the above-mentioned legal order, nor can the norms of their national law clash with the law deriving from the EEC Treaty without losing their communitarian character and questioning the juridical basis of the Community. In particular, the European judge remarked that the efficacy of European law cannot vary from one State to another due to subsequent internal statutes without questioning the scopes of the Treaty and causing citizenship discrimination[7]. The Italian Constitutional Court – prior to the Maastricht Treaty – despite its disagreements with the thesis of the Court of Justice of the EU according to which the normative sources of the Community and those of the single States are to be considered as parts of the same system, reached the conclusion, as we know, that "*the Italian judge will always apply community regulations, even when prior or subsequent conflicting dispositions are present in the national law*."[8] In fact, community regulations are meant to guarantee egalitarian conditions both among the States and their citizens before the functioning mode of the legal order and the organization of the Common Market itself.

Thus, it does not seem to be relevant whether the citizens of the EU will constitute one single people in the traditional meaning of the term or not because the current nature of the European Union is not that of a general-purpose body. As Art. 2 of the current Treaty of Lisbon[9] on the EU highlights – through a "super-norm" of the European legal system – the common values on which the EU is based constitute the premise for a gradual formation of a wider new *demos* through a process of social and political integration among the different European peoples in compliance

6 ECJ, *Van Gend & Loos*, C-26/62, ECR 1963, 00003.

7 This conclusion is consolidated in European jurisprudence: ECJ, *RS*, C-430/21, ECLI:EU:C:2022:44; ECJ, *Euro Box Promotion*, C-357/19, C-379/19, C-547/19, C-811/19 and C-840/19, ECLI:EU:C:2021:1034 246.

8 See Italian Constitutional Court, *Granital*, no. 170 of 1984 [translation by the author].

9 Treaty of Lisbon – Amending the Treaty on European Union and the Treaty Establishing The European Community, O.J. C 306/1.

with the principals of equality and non-discrimination.[10] In fact, according to a broad European legal order, EU citizenship is destined to become the essential status of all citizens of the Member States (be they active or inactive from an economic standpoint[11]). It will allow persons with similar situations to get, within the scope of application of the Treaty[12], the same juridical treatment independently of their national belonging, except where explicitly provided for otherwise.[13]

Indeed, we can envision a "community of law" only if we assume that – to put it in the words of the Advocate General *M. Poiares Maduro* – though such citizenship is complementary to the national ones and not substitutive of them, it represents the "*basis of a new political space from which rights and duties arise that are fixed by the communitarian law and are not dependent on the single States*"[14].

B. *Its "independent structure" with respect to national citizenships*

If it is true that European citizenship entails the citizenship of one of the Member States and that, according to the Amsterdam Treaty[15], the former does not substitute the latter but complements it, the juridical and political notion that arises from the European status can be qualified as "independent" from the respective national belongings; as the Court of Justice has

10 For those notations, please refer to *Castorina*, I valori fondanti dell'Unione europea, Riflessioni sul processo costituente europeo, 2010, p. 391.

11 See the Opinion of Advocate General Szpunar, *Sean Ambrose McCarthy Helena Patricia McCarthy Rodriguez Natasha Caley McCarthy Rodriguez* v *Secretary of State for the Home Department*, C-202/13, ECLI:EU:C2014:345, no. 39.

12 Among the situations that fall within the scope of application of Community law there are those concerning the exercise of the fundamental freedoms guaranteed by the Treaty and, in particular, the freedom to move and reside within the territory of the Member States: now, see Art. 21 TFEU.

13 Among the first rulings of the Luxembourg Court, in this regard, ECJ, *Grzelczyk*, C-184/99, ECR 2001, I-06193, no. 31; ECJ, *D´Hoop*, C-224/98, ECR 2002, I-06191, no. 28; ECJ, *Garcia Avello,* C-148/02, ECR 2003, I-11613, no. 22 f.; ECJ, *Pusa*, C-224/02, ECR 2004, I-05763, no. 16. With the *Martínez Sala* judgment (ECJ, *Martinez Sala*, C-85/96, ECR 1998, I-02691) the Court recognized European citizenship as having direct effect in the context of social security.

14 Opinion of Advocate General Poiares Maduro, *Janko Rottmann* v *Freistaat Bayern.* C-135/08, ECR 2010, I-01449.

15 Treaty of Amsterdam Amending the Treaty on European Union, The Treaties Establishing the European Communities and Related Acts, O.J. C 340/1.

recently pointed out, such citizenship exists as long as the political bond among the Member State and the Union is operative.[16]

In fact, those two notions are inextricably connected and autonomous at the same time, as *Maduro* points out, since they are kept together by political ties that bring European peoples together into a single area of rights and duties based on the mutual commitment to open the respective political communities to other European citizens and build a new form of political and civic solidarity on a European scale.[17]

European citizenship, however, is not an "*empty shell*"[18] and a true political community would be unthinkable without a form of common belonging in terms of identity. The latter is the foundation of a political space from which rights and duties for the citizens of the Member States arise (Art. 17 para. 2 Maastricht Treaty): from this point of view, it has been very much appreciated by the jurisprudence of the Court of Justice especially for its essential core consisting in the principle of national non-discrimination (Art. 12 Maastricht Treaty). The consequences of this principle follow two main trajectories.

On the one hand, from the above-mentioned principle stems the right to equal treatment within the single Member States reserved to all their citizens who share a similar condition; on the other, as the Court of Justice underlined[19], citizens of the Member States are entitled to the treatment

16 ECJ, *EP* v *Préfet du Gers, Institut national de la statistique et des études économiques,* C-673/20, ECLI:EU:C:2022:449. The Court clarified that, since the withdrawal of the United Kingdom from the European Union (1 Feb. 2020), British citizens who transferred their residence to a Member State before the end of the transition period, would no longer benefit from the status of citizen of the Union nor, in particular, from the right to vote and participate in municipal elections in the Member State of residence, even if they are also deprived, by virtue of the law of the State of which they are citizens, of the right to vote in elections called by that same State.

17 Opinion of Advocate General Poiares Maduro (fn. 14), no. 23. On the principle of solidarity, see more recently the ECJ, *Federal Republic of Germany, Republic of Poland* v *European Commission and others*, C-848/19, ECLI:EU:C:2021:598.

18 The expression is found in Opinion of Advocate General Wathelet, *Secretary of State for the Home Department* v *NA*, C-115/15, ECLI:EU:C:2016:259, no. 111.

19 ECJ, *Herbert Schwarz, Marga Gootjes-Schwarz and Finanzamt Bergisch Gladbach*, C-76/05, ECR 2007, I-06849, no. 88 ff., in which a national legislation is declared incompatible with Union law because it introduces a difference in treatment between taxpayers, subject to income tax in Germany, who educate their children in a school located in Germany and those who send their children to study in a school located in another Member State, not granting them the same tax benefits, thus disadvantaging their own citizens simply because they have exercised their freedom to move and reside in another Member State and restricting the rights recognized to all EU citizens

set by their national legal order when they decide to exercise their right to freedom of movement and residence provided for by the Maastricht Treaty.

The principle of non-discrimination follows two different trajectories that work alongside with the independent structure of the European citizenship in relation to the single national citizenships: externally, that is, it does not allow unequal treatment towards the citizens of the hosting Member State when the rights provided for by the Treaties are exercised, especially the right to free movement and residence; internally, that is, it does not allow discrimination against persons who claim protection and ask for integration in their own Member State when the rights provided for by the Treaties are exercised.[20] To this regard, the Court of Justice pointed out that Art. 20 TFEU holds back national measures that prevent European citizens from truly enjoying the rights arising from their status because of their possibility to appeal to the rights deriving from their supranational citizenship even against the Member States of their belonging.[21]

To sum up, both within the European and national spheres, the autonomy of the European citizenship entitles its beholders to the so-called "original rights".[22] Such citizenship can be interpreted as an actual "condition of the person" that does not tolerate – neither within a hosting Member State nor within a citizen's State of belonging – exceptions to the formal equality before the law (Art. 3 of the Italian Constitution). European law can justify such exceptions, as we know, only when considerations that are objective and adequately proportionate to the aim pursued within the single Member States exist, which do not depend solely on the national citizenship of the person involved.

The broad progress in terms of integration that has been made so far confirms the idea that a "true Union" requires a true overcoming of all in-

---

by the Art. 18 of the Treaty on European Union. In this circumstance, the Court clarified that the courses taught by the educational institutions, which are mainly financed by private funds (in particular by pupils or their parents), constitute services pursuant to Art. 50 of the above mentioned Treaty because the aim of the educational institutions is to offer a service in exchange for a fee.

20 See the Opinion of Advocate General Szpunar, *Alfredo Rendón Marín* v *Administración del Estado,* C-165/14, ECLI:EU:C:2016:75, no. 116.

21 See ECJ, *Ruiz Zambrano*, C-34/09, ECR 2011, I-01177, no. 42, but also ECJ, *McCarthy*, C-434/09, ECR 2011, I-03375, no. 48; ECJ, *Dereci and others*, C-256/11, ECR 2011, I-11315, no. 63, as well as ECJ, *O and others*, C-356/11 and C-357/11, ECLI:EU:C2012:595, no. 44.

22 ECJ, *Secretary of State for the Home Department* v *CS*, C-304/14, ECLI:EU:C:2016:75, no. 28.

equalities among the citizens of the Member States through the promotion of economic and social cohesion. In this regard, we can say that the status of European citizenship is to be fundamentally appreciated in the light of the progressive and dynamic character of the integration movement of individuals and States towards a "community of law".[23]

C. The health crisis and the economic crisis: a contradictory trend in European citizenship

The recent pandemic and economic crises that struck the entire continent have brought about the topic of European citizenship, stressing its contradictory development: on the one hand, it has registered a remarkable signal of appreciation for a so-called "more social" integration within the European Union; whereas on the other, it has laid bare that on a European scale, we miss shared and consolidated reference values that would transform integration into a joint process.

In particular, the Covid-19 pandemic and the so-called "conditionality regime" – according to which, the disbursement of funds from the European budget depends on positive feedback on compliance with the Rule of Law – can be indicated, in order, as the occasion that reinforced a broader trust in a European Union, which appears as more sensitive and proactive towards the essential needs of European citizens; the conditionality regime, in its turn, highlighted obstacles in the definition of a common European identity based on the liberal contents of the civic understanding of citizenship and generally shared institutional values. The reason for that is the consistent violation of the Rule of Law – which in some Member States can even be considered systemic – that is able to seriously interfere with a sound financial management of the EU and cause damage to a number of citizens and enterprises[24].

23 *Closa*, The concept of citizenship in the Treaty on European Union, Common Market Law Review 29 (1992), 1137 (1167).

24 *European Commission*, Communication from the Commission to the European Parliament, the Council, the European economic and social Committee and the Committee of the Regions 2023. Rule of Law Report, The rule of law situation in the European Union, COM/2023/800 final, 5 July 2023.

D. The Coronavirus pandemic and the "opening" of the Union towards a European system of multilevel solidarity

The Covid-19 crisis brought the organization of the social State in Europe to its knees already during the first months of 2020: the healthcare system – which has been subject to sever economic depotentiation over the last few years, in order to ensure compliance with the European restrictions (among other reasons) – has suffered dramatic solicitations as it had already happened in other important welfare sectors – such as the labor market, education and social support to tackle inequalities.

As a consequence of the pandemic experience, during the Porto Social Summit of 7-8 May 2021, the European Council discussed the mechanisms of reinforcement of the European social rights, hoping for more efficient coordination between the Member States and the European institutions.

The final Declaration of the Porto Social Summit stressed unity and European solidarity in facing Covid-19. Participants agreed that it was necessary to move with more resolution towards a "social Europe" that would take into consideration the ongoing changes in people's lifestyle and consumption habits as well as on the labor market, without forgetting the digital and green transitions. The purpose for it all is to achieve a "collective recovery" by strengthening the social dimension of the integration process in coherence with the 2017 European Pillar of social rights.[25]

While the European institutions were dealing with the pandemic crisis, European citizenship proved that its structure is independent from the single national belongings. By taking on the task of procuring Covid-19 vaccines on the international market on behalf of the Member States – in the execution of Commission's Decision 4192 final of 18 June 2020 – the EU showed that with respect to public health, it made room within the European legal order for the development of the social dimension of integration, without prejudice to the Treaties. In fact, the EU gained an important "participation share" in guaranteeing the fundamental rights that are still reserved to the Member States: the present state of European integration allows citizens of the Member States to cherish concrete expectations regarding the direct protection of their wellbeing solely with regard to their State of belonging.

---

25 In particular, in the final Declaration: "*More than ever, Europe must be the continent of social cohesion and prosperity. We reaffirm our commitment to working towards a social Europe.*"

It is worth noting that in the Communication on the EU Covid-19 Vaccines Strategy[26], the Commission presented the EU strategy – meant to accelerate the development, fabrication and dissemination of the Covid-19 vaccine – as a direct initiative to "contribute to the protection of all persons, especially of the EU citizens". Thus, as a response to the weakness of the Member States in providing efficient national solutions to the ever-growing sanitary crisis, the EU carried out a relevant activity aimed at supporting and integrating the health-care systems of its Member States. As a consequence, the European institutions were endowed with a "more human" face while handling the direct protection of their citizens' wellbeing.

Hence, among the European citizens who declared themselves in favor of a more active role of the EU in the social sphere – as of the survey conducted by the European Parliament in June 2020 – the majority agreed that the EU should have more competences to face the sanitary crisis and expressed their hope for a more adequate European budget to be destined to that purpose. Furthermore, the survey highlighted that the Member States gave proof of poor solidarity while dealing with the pandemic crisis.[27]

Regardless of the results of the survey, Europe's response to the sanitary emergency proved to operate according to a logic of solidarity and cooperation rather than an intergovernmental one: from a position of independence from national governments, the Commission promoted actions aimed at the protection of public health ascribable to the EU as a whole, although the latter does not hold either shared or exclusive competence for the protection of health, since such protection falls into the sphere of sovereign competence of the Member States[28].

26 European Commission, 17 June 2020, COM(2020) 245 final.

27 See *European Parliament*, Citizens call for a bigger EU budget to tackle crisis, available at: www.europarl.europa.eu/at-your-service/it/be-heard/eurobarometer/public-opinion-in-the-eu-in-time-of-coronavirus-crisis-2 (last access: 23 Oct 2025).

28 It is known that, with specific regard to medicinal products and devices for medical use, the TFEU – in the context of "common safety problems in the field of public health": Art. 4 (2) lit. k TFEU; Art. 168 (4) lit. c TFEU – attributes to the Union a competence shared with the Member States solely with regard to the setting of high quality and safety parameters, which mainly concern marketing authorizations. These authorizations are compulsory for vaccination devices and they are delivered by the European Commission following the opinion of the European Medicines Agency (EMA). More generally on this matter, and for the rest, the Union can only "support, coordinate or complement the actions of the Member States" (Art. 6 TFEU) with initiatives which, in the field of public health, are of limited scope, as they 'simply complement the actions of the Member States'. In fact, the Parliament and

The guiding role taken on by the Commission – it should be sufficient to think of the tactical supply of medical tools in the context of a reinforced "Civil Protection mechanism" born in 2001 with the aim of improving the prevention and management of catastrophes[29] – revealed a remarkable stance to overrule, without prejudice to the Treaties, the deeply-rooted concepts of "residuality" and "instrumentality" of the social rights in relation to the financial goals of the Common Market. The above-mentioned role shows remarkable openness towards a European system of multilevel solidarity.[30]

E. The economic conditionality clause and the "rupture" of the legal status *of European citizenship*

The expenditure of the European funds for the economic recovery, which is conditioned on compliance with the principles of the Rule of Law, determines the denial of the rights deriving from the Union's budget to a number of European citizens.[31]

The clause of economic conditionality, pursuant Regulation 2020/2092, as we know, is aimed at safeguarding the financial interests of the Union, yet it contradicts the idea of European citizenship as a status whose structure is independent from the single national citizenships, in case a Member State is not considered to be respectful of the values on which the Union is based

---

the Council have prerogatives that tend to be "weak" and non-legislative, one could say, incentivizing, as it is the case of other sectors in which the same prohibition on the harmonization of the legislative and regulatory provisions of the national legal systems arises, sanctioned, in fact, in the Art. 168 (5) TFEU: remains, therefore, "without prejudice to the primary responsibility of the Member States to protect people, the environment and property, including cultural heritage, on their territory from disasters and to equip their respective disaster management systems with sufficient means to adequately and consistently deal with disasters of a reasonably foreseeable nature and scale and for which they can be prepared".

29 See https://ec.europa.eu/commission/presscorner/detail/it/ip_20_476 (last access: 23 Oct 2025).

30 *Castorina*, L'approvvigionamento centralizzato dei vaccini nell'U.E.: verso un sistema multilivello dei diritti sociali, Questioni di diritto costituzionale nell'epidemia globale, 2023, p. 49 ff.

31 *Castorina*, Il Piano per la ripresa tra condizionalità economica e rispetto dello Stato di diritto, Questioni di diritto costituzionale, p. 95 ff.

(Art. 2 TEU) in areas that fall under the exclusive competence of the State, such as the administration of justice.[32]

According to the Court of Justice, compliance with the values of the Rule of Law cannot be reduced to a duty forced on a candidate State before joining the EU, which it can elude after its adhesion.[33]

The economic conditionality clause ends up weakening the solidarity bond among the peoples of the Union, one of the fundamental principles of the European legal order on which common citizenship is based.[34]

As we can notice, the direct protection of well-being during the pandemic crisis and the conditionality clause, in order to face dangerous national deviations from the principle of Rule of Law, have revealed a contradictory and imperfect unity status. European citizenship, in fact, presents weak boundaries due to the incompleteness of the European constituent project. On the one hand, the latter shows "openness" towards the vital needs of the European society and its citizens; whereas on the other, it makes the ability of the European citizens to fully enjoy the economic resources deriving from the Union's budget dependent on the inner institutional conditions of the Member States, thus causing disparity of treatment among European citizens.

The values of the Rule of Law define European identity as a legal order. Hence, the Union is ready to defend them even at the cost of causing a rupture in the unity status of European citizenship. From this point of view, however, only a more advanced integration would be able to justify deeper control of the European bodies over the respect of the constitutional lawfulness of the Member States, truly departing from "a European standpoint": to do so, it would be necessary to take the path of constitutionalisation and federalization of the Union, that is to say, resort to the proceeding foreseen under Art. 7 TEU. This proceeding represents the most arduous but also the most appropriate tool to address the deprivation of the rights deriving from the application of the Treaties because it brings about aspects of "non-shared sovereignty" reserved to the exclusive competence of the

32 *Castorina*, I valori fondanti dell'Unione europea, in Riflessioni sul processo costituente europeo, 2010, p. 387.

33 See ECJ, *Republic of Poland* v *European Parliament, Council of the European Union,* C-157/21, ECLI:EU:C:2021:978, no. 140 ff.; similarly ECJ, *Hungary* v *European Parliament, Council of the European Union*, C-156/21, ECLI:EU:C:2021:97.

34 See ECJ, *Germany* v *Republic of Poland*, C-848/19, ECLI:EU:C:2021:598, no. 38 ff.

European Counsel with unanimous resolution of the Heads of State and government.[35]

F. From the "ecological crisis" to a relaunch of European citizenship?

Against this uncertain background, we can see signals of revival of the European citizenship in the process that started in 2019 with the *Green Deal*[36], in line with the Paris Agreement on climate change (2015)[37]. The *Green Deal* indicates the goals of sustainable development and climate neutrality, which cannot be pursued without seriously rethinking the lifestyle of individuals and local communities. The so-called "green citizenship" may represent an important starting point for the enrichment of European citizenship with new dimensions of identification and democratic participation in pursuing common goals.[38]

As the European Commission pointed out, the *Green Deal* provides for the involvement of the civil society and the active participation of the European citizens. The latter will be favored by setting up physical and virtual spaces where citizens will have the opportunity to express their ideas, with the perspective of making energy production and everyone's lifestyles less harmful for the environment. Thus, people's welfare and fundamental rights will be put at the center of economic policies.

Hence, sustainable development requires "*a new pact* [...] *to bring together citizens in all their diversity, with national, regional, local authorities, civil society and industry working closely with the EU's institutions and consultative bodies.*"[39] For those reasons, European citizens are indicated as the "*driving force of the transition*"[40] and are invested "*to act* [...] *together*"[41] with awareness of the fact that global ecological issues, along with equally

---

35 *Castorina*, Il "federalismo imperfetto dell'Unione europea" e il rispetto dei principi dello Stato di diritto, Rivista giuridica Ambiente Diritto.it, 2021.

36 See *European Commission,* Communication to the European Parliament, the European Council, the Council, the European economic and social committee and the Committee of the Regions. The European Green Deal, 11 Dec 2019, COM(2019) 640 final.

37 Paris Agreement, UNTS 3156, p. 79.

38 For further reference see *Amand/Jareño Cuesta* (eds.), The future of Environmental Citizenship in the EU, 2021, p. 27.

39 See *European Commission* (fn. 36).

40 *Ibid.*

41 *Ibid.*

important ongoing challenges (e.g. migratory phenomena, public safety), question the classic model of citizenship inherited from liberal Revolutions and essentially based on economic rights.[42] Such issues put forward a new model that considers the shared belonging to the Union not as a "passive" or "private" status[43], but as an active practice, in which rights go hand in hand with duties and virtues.[44] In this context, eco-compatible behaviors enter seamlessly the legal order along with other virtuous behavior patterns of Western democratic societies (such as recycling, the purchase of local biological products and the use of public transportation)[45].

As the European Climate Law establishes[46], individuals and communities will have to play a decisive role in pursuing "green goals", established to protect, preserve and improve the Union's natural heritage as well as safeguard the wellbeing of its citizens from environmental and climate risks. Such goals are supported by an ever-growing awareness, on a national level, regarding a specific constitutional commitment to guarantee the interests of future generations with regard to the environment, biodiversity and ecosystems[47] (see Art. 9 para. 3 of the Italian Constitution, added in 2022).

To conclude, the *Green Deal* and the implementation of the European Pillar of Social Rights can jointly start the strategy for a social market economy (Art. 3 para. 3, TEU) that could allow the EU to become "*a fair, healthy, sustainable and prosperous society*"[48] and a "*resilient economy that*

42 *Isin/Wood*, Citizenship and identity, 1999, 114; *M.J. Smith/Pangsapa*, Environment and citizenship: Integrating justice, responsibility and civic engagement, 2008, p. 9.

43 *Kymlicka/Norman*, Return of the Citizen: A Survey of Recent Work on Citizenship Theory, Ethics 104(2) (1994), 352.

44 *Machin/Tan*, Green European citizenship? Rights, duties, virtues, practices and the European Green Deal, European politics and society 25 (2024), 152 (155).

45 See *Certomà*, Questione Ambientale e Transizione Ecologica, https://web.uniroma1.it, p. 4, referring to Dobson's approach (*Dobson*, Citizenship and the environment, 2003), according to whom ecological citizenship focuses on duties and rights. Such duties apply, in a non-reciprocal way, to individuals and communities that occupy unsustainable amounts of ecological space to those who occupy too little.

46 Regulation (EU) 2021/1119 of the European Parliament and of the Council of 30 June 2021, establishing the framework for achieving climate neutrality and amending Regulations (EC) No 401/2009 and (EU) 2018/1999 ('European Climate Law').

47 The valorization of which also implies the fight against climate change, cf. *Bifulco*, Ambiente e cambiamento climatico nella Costituzione italiana, Rivista AIC 3 (2023), 132.

48 See *European Commission*, Communication to the European Parliament, the Council, the European economic and social committee and the Committee of the Regions. European Climate Pact, 9 Dec 2020, COM(2020) 788 final.

works for people and for nature"[49]. This program is certainly ambitious, but it could broaden the range of social rights on which the principle of non-discrimination based on nationality can act especially in the field of the fruition of public services. In this perspective, the direct intervention of the Union in the matter of social rights can be more effective, as we have already seen in the case of the protection of public and private health.

Against this background, citizenship shows ever more inclusive potential for establishing one sole European *demos*, while a decisive progress towards a federal European community of law still appears as a distant perspective.

49 *Ibid.*

Authors

Bond, Niall	Associate Professor, University Lyon II, France and Research Associate, Sociology Department, University of Johannesburg, South Africa.
Castorina, Emilio	Prof. Dr., University of Catania, Italy.
Hofmann, Rainer	Prof. Dr. Dr., Goethe-University Frankfurt am Main, Germany.
Kadelbach, Stefan	Prof. Dr., LL.M. (University of Virginia), Goethe-University Frankfurt am Main, Germany.
Kovács, Kriszta	Associate Professor, ELTE University, Human Rights and Politics Department, Budapest, Hungary and Visiting Research Fellow, Wissenschaftszentrum Berlin für Sozialforschung, Berlin, Germany.
Lipowicz, Irena	Prof. Dr., Wyszynski-University of Warsaw and former Polish Ambassador to Austria, Poland.
Simon, Sven	Prof. Dr., Philipps-University Marburg, Germany and Member of the European Parliament, Strasbourg, France.
Žaltauskaitė-Žalimienė, Skirgailė	Prof., PhD, Vilnius University and President of the Supreme Administrative Court of Lithuania, Lithuania.